"Tonight We Fly!"

The Soviet Night Witches

of

WWII

Claudia Hagen

ISBN - 13: 978-1543036671
ISBN - 10: 154-3036678

All quoted material comes from a variety of interviews, reports, documents, news stories, magazine articles, videos, websites, and/or books listed in the bibliography.

All photographs, unless otherwise credited, were obtained by accessing public domain archives.

Front and back covers designed and created by
Marty Bicek, Bicek Photography - Modesto, California.
Copyright 2017 by Marty Bicek.

Dedicated to the early military aviation women worldwide who fought courageously for their countries in times of struggle and war then were neglected and forgotten in the pages of history.

Without these brave women of yesteryear marking trails in the sky, we would not have the outstanding women pilots of today serving military, commercial, and private aviation worldwide.

Table of Contents

Table of Contents (continued)

Introduction

While researching my last book, *American Women During WWII,* I came across an interesting article about the young women flying combat missions for the Soviet Union during World War II. Once again, it should be noted that the history of any war always includes women; however, their accomplishments are not highly recognized, recorded, nor remembered. After my book was published, I began a further study of these remarkable women and their amazing history very few Americans are aware of.

Soviet-era Communism embraced the equality of the sexes with nearly one million Soviet women serving on the front lines as anti-aircraft gunners, snipers, bombers, and fighter pilots. Their fighter and bomber pilots were the only women flying combat missions from any of the countries involved in WWII. The Soviet women were the first in fighter and bomber planes, the first in front line combat, and the first to be honored with their nation's highest military honors. Most were young, in their late teens and early twenties, adventurous, had a love of flying, and were patriotic to their country. By 1941, between one-fourth and one-third of all Soviet pilots were female - a small but mighty percentage, as you will see.

Just as the American women with a desire to serve their country during wartime experienced, the Soviet women also had a rough start in being taken seriously or accepted for their wartime efforts. It did not take long before either country's women proved their worth and established their unique and unmatched place in the history of that time. The problem was, and still is, not many knew about the Soviet women and the amazing achievements they had accomplished. This might be due, in part, to postwar activities and hostilities between the Soviet Union, the United States and many other nations. News or information received by Westerners regarding Soviet women fighter pilots or combatants was likely passed off as Soviet propaganda and ignored. Soviet arrogance was also found to have distorted many historical facts from that time period.

With few resources, outdated equipment, and laughable aircraft, the Soviet women became the first "stealth bombers" in the truest sense of the term, and were some of the most feared pilots during the war. The women pilots relentlessly harassed the German strongholds in the dark of night by dropping bombs on them unexpectedly, thus not allowing the soldiers any nighttime rest or recovery. The Germans despised them and placed bounties on them. Hitler awarded any German soldier who downed one, the highly coveted Iron Cross medal. They were convinced the women were given special vitamins, medicines or injections by the Soviet government to give them catlike, night vision. Untrue!

As the night flyers approached their targets they would cut their engines, glide down silently, drop their bombs, restart their engines, pull up sharply, return to base, rearm and fly to their next mission. These attacks continued until the dark night sky turned to the predawn light of sunrise.

When the small planes glided to their targets, a soft whooshing sound could be heard as the air passed through their rickety aircraft. The sound may have been like the perceived fairy tale of a witch flying a broomstick through the night sky. In turn, the Germans called them *Nachtexen* which roughly translated to Night Witches.

As I began to gather information about these fearless women, it quickly became apparent that stories were conflicted and conflicting, facts and figures differed, and that I knew very little Soviet history - specifically what or why these fearless women would put themselves in these death defying positions with rattle-trap aircraft.

The Soviets have always guarded their historical facts from the rest of the world with secrecy, egotism and a dash of insolence concerning anything in general, nothing in particular. Only in recent years with changes in leadership have bits and pieces become more readily available to outside historians, researchers, even the Soviet people themselves. Thus, a large part of my research had to include learning a bit of Soviet history then constantly sorting facts from fiction and perceived propaganda.

Facts and figures have been carefully evaluated from multiple sources and utilized in this book. Notations are made where conflicts could not be resolved utilizing multiple sources. All sources are listed in the bibliography.

Introduction

Although history may be a bit boring to some, many Americans know very little about the Soviets and their WWII history. America and the Soviet Union were allies during WWII; not so much afterwards. Many of us grew up fearing them during the Cold War years as we crouched under our desks during atomic bomb drills in school or family bomb shelters built in the back yard.

Soviet history is complicated and sometimes confusing; therefore, I have only touched on the history here as it pertains to setting the scene, the Night Witches, and their part in WWII.

One person of special interest mentioned throughout this book and throughout Soviet history is Marina Raskova. Marina has been called the Soviet counterpart to American Amelia Earhart. Both made significant contributions to women's aviation by setting examples and empowering young girls and women to take to the skies. Both continue to be recognized today as pioneers and heroes in the history of women's aviation.

Informational stories about individual women pilots have been gleaned from a variety of sources. Actual dialogue appearing between quotation marks or with italics has been conveyed via biographies, written interviews, memoirs, films, videos, or news articles. Conjecture may have been used to enhance descriptions based on factual information. Author's notes in italics are informational or provide clarification within the text. All photographs, unless otherwise credited, were obtained from accessing public domain archives. I have also avoided the distraction of footnotes and chapter notes; instead, detailed source information has been included in the body of the text wherever possible. All sources are listed in the bibliography at the end of the book.

It is my hope to bring to the reader an understanding of the great historical significance of these Soviet women and the amazing role they played in WWII.

Chapter 1

U.S.S.R., Soviets, Russians?

Volatile. Variable. Confusing. The history is definitely confusing to many Westerners who were daydreaming or fell asleep in World History 101 or Political Science 202 classes. What's the difference between the U.S.S.R., the Soviet Union, and Russia? Are the citizens called Russians or are they called Soviets? Let me try to explain it all in the simplest of terms.

The Union of Soviet Socialist Republics (U.S.S.R.) existed from 1922 to 1991 and was often referred to simply/commonly as the Soviet Union. The Union was made up of multiple republics such as Kazakstan, Moldova, Belarus, Ukraine, and Russia. The citizens of the Soviet Union were called Soviets under the Communist rule but retained their republic ethnicity, i.e. Ukrainian, Moldovian, Russian, etc. Think about it in this comparative way: the United States of America is made up of a collective of 50 states each with its own government yet under Federal laws; California, New York, Iowa, etc. Citizens of each state are called Californians, New Yorkers, Iowans, but collectively referred to as Americans.

When the Soviet economy collapsed in the 1990s, fourteen republics became independent of one another. Russia, the largest republic, became its own country as did the smaller republics. Russia covers more than one-eighth of the Earth's inhabited land area and today is the world's ninth most populous country. Herein lies the confusion for many. A number of folks say/think that Russia is the same as the Soviet Union under a new name. It is not. That would be like saying New York or California is the United States of America after the U.S.A. was dissolved and each state became independent.

During World War II (WWII) the Soviet Union soldiers were usually referred to as Soviets, Russians, or "Commies" (Communists) by those trying to invade their country. The name Soviets and Russians were often used interchangeably during that period due to the fact that the ethnic Russians outnumbered any of the others from the smaller republics.

To be politically and historically correct for the time period conveyed throughout this book, the term Soviet(s) will be utilized when discussing the Soviet Union people as a whole, while the term Russian will be utilized only when discussing a person of Russian ethnicity.

The reader will also note the names of Soviet/Russian individuals can be tongue twisters! The first name is most often a shortened version of the patronymic (father or ancestor) name with an ending corresponding with gender. The last name is the family name. For example, the patronymic first name of Alexandrovna would mean "daughter of Alexander" shortened to Anna or Anya. The "a" denotes a female, "o" for a male.

Abbreviations are commonly used when referring to Soviet institutions or describing authoritative positions. The abbreviated term is formed by using the first syllables of the longer version. For example: *zampolit* is an abbreviated word for **zam**estitel *komandira po **polit**rabotye.* The shorter version has a broader meaning (a type of military commissar) than the longer version which is more specific (deputy commander of political work).

Military terminology during this time period may also be confusing. Whether the military branch was Air Force, Army or Navy, the Soviets used army terms and designations for all. The nomenclature most commonly used was armies, divisions, regiments, squadrons, units. Each army or military branch had divisions. Each division had three to five regiments. Each regiment had two to five squadrons. Each squadron had a number of units.

Military ranking for men and women in all branches was commander, major general, lieutenant general, colonel general, etc. Within each branch the designations would read, for example: commander of the regiment, major general of the air force, lieutenant general of the air force, etc.

There are frequent references to the Motherland or Mother Russia. The term Motherland is a symbol to the Soviet people just as Uncle Sam is a symbol to the American people.

Hopefully the reader is less confused about the terminology! Undoubtedly, history is boring to many readers. But, in order to understand the plight of the Soviet citizens during this time period, it is important to trudge through a bit of their history. Read on!

Chapter 2

The Great Patriotic War

The term World War II (WWII) was somewhat unfamiliar to the citizens of the former Soviet Union. Instead, the term The Great Patriotic War, was and still is commonly used when referring to and describing the war from June 22, 1941 to May 9, 1945 between the Soviet Union and Nazi Germany. Outside of these areas, the war between the Soviets and the Germans was generally known as the Eastern Front of WWII. Historians call The Great Patriotic War the worst battle in the history of humanity due to the incredible loss of life for all countries involved.

In the early months of 1941, both the United States and the Soviet Union had somewhat comparable civilian populations, although the Soviet Union had a much larger land mass. The U.S. population was at 133 million; the Soviet Union at 196 million. There was very little comparison of military figures between the two countries during that time. The U.S. had over 16 million serving in the military, while the Soviet Union had nearly 34 million serving.

By the war's end in late 1945, the death tolls between the two countries were devastating. The U.S. military suffered losses of over 400,000 killed in action; 670,000 were wounded; 18,000 taken as prisoners of war (*these figures do not include American troops killed in the Pacific theater*). There are over 73,000 U.S. soldiers still missing to this day. There were no civilian deaths as a result of combat on American soil; however, six citizens died while on a picnic in an Eastern Oregon forest. On May 5, 1945, a small family group came upon a Japanese balloon bomb caught in the brush. The bomb exploded as they approached killing five children and a pregnant woman. A small monument was later erected on the site by Weyerhaeuser Company at the Mitchell Recreation Area in Lake County, Oregon.

Weyerhaeuser monument at the site of Japanese balloon bomb explosion killing six May 5, 1945.

The exact figures for the Soviet Union have been disputed by various sources, however the following figures are generally accepted: nearly 9 million military personnel were killed; over 22 million wounded; over 4 million missing and presumed dead or taken as prisoners of war. Over one million Soviet prisoners of war were released after the war suffering from starvation and diseases and soon died. Over 18 million Soviet civilians were killed by extermination, famine/starvation, or death in Soviet forced labor camps.

Joseph Stalin was the dictatorial leader of the Soviet Union from 1929 to 1953. He ruled with brutal terror, eliminating anyone who opposed him. The Soviet Union had long been an agrarian or agricultural society with citizens producing and maintaining their own crops, livestock and farmland. Stalin changed that way of life shortly after coming into power. He took a firm grip on the economy by forcing the consolidation of individual peasant households into collective farms called *kolkhozes*. All land, livestock and equipment was seized by the government, but the citizens were still required to work the land, produce the foodstuffs and turn all over to the governmental authorities. Failure to comply would result in separation of women and children with deportation to the *Gulags,* brutal forced labor camps, or murder of the entire family. Young men and teens from the farms were often sent to serve in the military while the younger girls and women were sent to forced labor in the clothing or munitions factories.

Stalin also wanted the wealthier, more affluent farmers and landowners, *kulaks,* "liquidated as a class." Their wealth and land ownership was a threat to his power. If the kulaks did not willingly turn over their land, livestock and equipment they were arrested as traitors, murdered or deported to remote regions of the Soviet Union and forced to work in the labor camps. Most eventually died from starvation, frostbite and/or disease.

Food production for the entire nation was seriously disrupted due to Stalin's plans and led to unrest, uprisings, sabotage of land and livestock, and eventually nationwide famine. Millions of the farmers and their families who had publicly opposed collectivization were murdered or sent to forced labor camps. Bitterness and hatred of the Stalin regime carried over from generation to generation.

From an agrarian society, Stalin launched a period of industrialization. Some historians mark this period as the revolutionizing of the Soviet Union. By the late 1930s, just prior to the breakout of war, the Soviets had achieved world dominance in ore extraction (copper and manganese), synthetic rubber production, oil production, steel, cast iron, aluminum, coal, and cement production. Tractors, combines, trucks, heavy equipment, and defense supplies were rolling out of factories at an unprecedented rate. Railroads expanded into the far reaches of the vast country and infrastructure in the larger cities improved.

All of these production achievements came at a high price to the workers. Since many workers were peasants who had lost their farms to collectivization and had no skills or education, it was difficult for them to assimilate to factory work or heavy labor. Many were weak from hunger or starving from the lack of food, clean water, and common decency. If they could not keep up the pace, turn out quality goods free from errors, they were shot on the spot, their bodies dragged away, and another worker moved into the empty space. Millions of citizens continued to be brutally murdered either in the factories or labor camps on a daily basis.

Author's note: Various sources give conflicting numbers, however, it is estimated that between twenty to sixty million non-military Soviet citizens suffered "unnatural deaths" during Stalin's entire reign due to outright murder, execu-

tions, incarceration for bogus charges, torture, famine, or death in forced labor camps.

In January 1939, a buildup of military tanks, aircraft and munitions began. By June 1940, the Soviets began a seven day per week, ten to twelve hours per day work schedule. Stalin prepared for war by instilling more fear and terror into the citizens. Penalties for tardiness, not meeting quotas, or poor work quality meant prison time in the Gulags. As war became imminent, one-eighth of the Soviet industrial and strategic assets were quickly and quietly moved to the interior of the country; aircraft and munitions factories were the first to be relocated.

As Stalin changed the history of the Soviet Union, his fondest secret dream was to invade and control Germany, eventually conquering Europe and spreading his brand of Communism throughout the world. All of his industrialization moves and military buildups were unknown to the outside world. Most countries were led to believe the Soviets were a peaceful, agrarian country incapable of military might. Little did anyone suspect the Stalin regime had quietly built a military superpower. His plan was to invade Germany on July 6, 1941 but Adolf Hitler beat him to the (front line) punch.

Adolf Hitler was the ruthless, murderous Nazi *Fuhrer,* dictator, of Germany from 1934 to 1945, a close counterpart of terror to Stalin. Hitler had similar dreams of con-

quering Europe and beyond by spreading his racially moti-
vated Nazi ideology. Hitler viewed the Jews, Soviets and
other nationalities as *Untermenschen*, sub-human, socially
undesirable and had to be exterminated. The Hitler regime
is responsible for the genocide of nearly 6 million Jews as
well as an estimated 19.3 million civilians and prisoners of
war.

On August 23, 1939, Hitler and Stalin met and signed
the German-Soviet Nonaggression Pact or the Molotov-
Ribbentrop Pact, much to the surprise of many world leaders. The Pact set forth the agreement between the two countries to take no military action against each other for a period of ten years. The Pact was a complete sham! Both leaders had ulterior motives.

Stalin viewed it as a stall tactic to remain on peaceful
terms with Germany while continuing to build Soviet military might for his planned July 1941 invasion. Hitler
viewed it as a way to invade Poland without Soviet inter-
ference then continue on with his plan to invade the Soviet
Union. Nine days later, while the signatures were likely still
wet, September 1, 1939, Hitler invaded Poland. Two days
later, September 3, Britain and France declared war on
Germany resulting in the initiation of WWII in Europe.

In early 1940, Hitler continued to build his military then
invaded Denmark, Norway, France, Luxembourg, the
Netherlands, and Belgium. It was then time to take the Soviet Union down by surprise invasion.

Shortly after the Nonaggressive Pact was signed, Stalin was advised by top officials of intelligence reports received from multiple, reliable sources that Hitler was planning an imminent invasion of the Soviet Union. Winston Churchill sent a top secret message warning Stalin of the danger of invasion by the Germans. With information from informed sources, the U.S. Secretary of State, Cordell Hull, also notified the Soviet ambassador of the planned invasion. The ambassador, in turn, notified Stalin. Regular and repeated warnings of an imminent attack were sent from American and British intelligence agencies. Soviet spies also sent warnings to Stalin's top administrators. Stalin ignored all reports instead, foolishly relied on the terms of the Pact. He did not trust Churchill or Hull and definitely did not trust Hitler, but he quietly ordered his military to ramp up production and be prepared, just in case.

Hitler and his military officers had been aggressively planning their attack on the unsuspecting Soviets all along, even prior to the Pact. In early 1941, Hitler ordered his generals to conduct the war against the Soviets as one of annihilation rather than capture and coercion. Prior to the planned attack date, a written Policy of Annihilation was given to every German soldier ordering them to "kill all potential leaders of (Soviet) society, all communists, Jews, Gypsies, guerrillas, saboteurs, and those capable of resistance."

On June 22, 1941, a date that lives in infamy for the Soviet people, Operation Barbarossa began. Hitler moved the largest surprise invasion force in the history of warfare into place along the 1,800 mile Soviet Union front. Over four million German and their allied soldiers, 3,350 German tanks, 7,200 artillery pieces, 2,770 aircraft, 600,000 motor vehicles, and 700,000 horses were in position and combat ready.

At 1:00 a.m., the Soviet military, stationed in various locations along the border ("just in case," via Stalin), was ordered to "bring all forces to combat readiness...avoid provocative actions of any kind." The Soviet troops numbered 5.5 million, with 14 million reserves still being trained, included 23,000 tanks that were not well maintained or equipped and 19,533 aircraft, many of which were old WWI leftovers (in 1941 the Soviet Air Force was recognized as the largest in the world, even though the majority of their aircraft were old and obsolete). Ammunition, motor vehicles and radios were in short supply.

At approximately 3:15 a.m., the invasion began with a German artillery barrage and bombing of major cities along the front. The German *Luftwaffe,* air force, bombers caught the Soviet Air Force completely by surprise as they attacked multiple airfields destroying over 2,000 fighter and bomber aircraft on the first day, with a total of 4,000 destroyed by the end of the first week.

Operation Barbarossa was the largest and swiftest military operation in human history. Within the first week the Germans advanced nearly two hundred miles into Soviet territory, killed, captured or wounded 600,000 Soviet troops. Even though the Soviets had more man power and equipment, they were ill-prepared, lacked leadership, training, readiness, and decent, up-to-date equipment.

Hitler's intent for the surprise attack was a swift defeat of the Soviets within a three to six month time period. That first week gave the false impression that his plan was on course. Unfortunately, he did not take into account the vastness of the country, the deadly winter weather ahead, supply problems, nor the scarcity of food for his troops. But most of all, Hitler did not expect the ferocity of the Soviet people fighting for their country. Much to the dismay of Hitler, the war between the Soviets and the Germans dragged on for nearly four years.

At noon on the day of the surprise attack, Soviet news agencies broadcast details of the invasion to the citizens by foreign minister Vyacheslav Molotov who stated *"...without a declaration of war, German forces fell on our country, attacked our frontiers in many places...The Red Army and the whole nation will wage a victorious Patriotic War for our beloved country, for honor, for liberty...our cause is just. The enemy will be beaten. Victory will be ours!"* Molotov encouraged the population's devotion to their Mother Nation rather than the Party as the stunned people across the nation tried to comprehend the surprising and devastating news.

The next day the Soviet newspaper *Pravda* published an article written by Yemelyan Yaroslavsky, titled "The Great Patriotic War of the Soviet People" with the intention of motivating the Soviet people to fight the Nazi invaders.

For two weeks Stalin remained stunned and demoralized by the attack while his military ministers and commanders scrambled to mobilize Red Army troops. During that time, Stalin ordered several of his top military officials executed for unauthorized military assignments that had not come from him directly nor had he initiated.

Stalin finally addressed the Soviet people on July 3, 1941 via radio. He called upon them to fight the invaders and used the term The Great Patriotic War, likely taken from Yaroslavsky's newspaper article.

Few of the nation's people supported Stalin and his ruthless ways. They looked upon the German invasion with hope for change and a return to a less brutal dictator. It did not take them long to realize that Hitler and the Nazi ideology was even worse than Stalin and his quests. German troops looted and burned villages, tortured and murdered the villagers especially the communists, Jews, and anyone with an education. All food stuffs were confiscated or burned, farm animals slaughtered, farm equipment destroyed and art or precious metals were taken and sent to Germany. These innocent people were a threat to Hitler's grandiose scheme of world domination and his quest for a

German "master race." He would achieve his master race through starvation and annihilation of the Soviet people.

The Great Patriotic War became a war of national survival to the Soviet people. They were unwilling to fight for their terrible dictator or the ruthless German dictator, instead the people, the common villagers and peasants in obscure regions, formed partisan groups. Their intent was to fight fiercely for freedom, independence, and survival to revenge the brutal murders of their relatives and defend their beloved Motherland.

The Soviet people were in a kill or be killed situation with the Germans. The Americans were in a similar situation with the Japanese after their own day of infamy, December 7, 1941.

The world was at war and would be changed forever.

Chapter 3

"Boys & Girls - Take up Aviation!"

The political history of the U.S.S.R. was ever changing under its various leaders and differing regimes. With each new leader came changes in the educational philosophies of Soviet youth. For example: Boy Scout and Girl Scout organizations became popular in 1910 with thousands of young children enjoying the Scout camaraderie and competitions; however, the Bolshevik regime promptly eliminated it. In 1918, a political youth organization was formed to instill political militancy in Soviet youth under then Communist revolutionary leader Vladimir Lenin. Lenin stressed the importance of political and military-style education of youth in building his new society. This group was known as the Russian Young Communist League, later changed to the All-Union Communist Party or the Communist Union of Youth but more commonly known as the Komsomol.

The Komsomol was the third stage in the hierarchy of Soviet youth organizations. The first group for youth aged seven to nine was the Little Octobrists, next up for youth aged ten to fifteen was the Young Pioneers. At age fourteen, both boys and girls were eligible to become a Komsomol member if their grades were in good standing and they had no "bad behavior" on their school records. Behavior problems often resulted in a term at one of the juvenile prisons to "correct" the problems. Children from very religious families were excluded from membership and were often sent to day labor camps instead. The Soviet doctrine at that time was one of atheism. Youth with aspirations for a career that would require a higher level of education, in order to be accepted by a college or military school, were expected to be a member in good standing of the Komsomol. Membership in Komsomol was valid until age twenty-eight.

In the Komsomol groups, the young people adhered to very strict policies of no smoking, no drinking, no religion, and definitely no activities resembling "hooliganism." The focus was on volunteer work, sports, and patriotism to the Motherland. In the Soviet Union, "voluntary" actually meant "partially obligatory" and applied to any and all citizens, young and old alike. Many young Komsomol members went on to become powerful political members of the Communist Party.

The Soviet government emphasized, through the youth organizations, the importance of physical fitness, paramilitary training, and aviation. Propaganda posters caught the attention of Soviet youth with captions reading, "Boys & Girls - Take up Aviation!" Marina Raskova also publicly encouraged girls to become involved with aviation, "Speaking as a pilot, I want more of our Soviet girls to study aviation and take to the skies."

Osoaviakhim (the Society for Cooperation in Defense and Aviation-Chemical Development) was a paramilitary sport organization for teens, young adults, and civilians, most of whom had aged out of the Komsomol. The focus for its members was on weapons, automobiles, and aviation. This group formed in 1927 training quasi-military skills such as defense, chemical warfare, glider flying and parachuting. Their goal was "patriotic upbringing of the population and preparation of it to the defense of the Motherland," very similar to Komsomol.

By 1930, the Osoaviakhim had developed a large network of air clubs across the region to provide flight training in light aircraft as well as aircraft maintenance, repair, navigation - anything related to or pertaining to aviation.

Since the Soviet Union was the first country in the world to proclaim legal equality for women, the air clubs could not exclude teen or young adult women from joining and learning to fly. They could, however, make it very difficult for them to go on and actually achieve the coveted pilot's license. Persistence and the strong desire of women Osoaviakhim members to become military pilots usually gained them entry into a military flight school. There they focused on flight training and military discipline. Graduates with high marks were awarded their pilot's license and an officer's rank.

In 1931, the Komsomol, through the Osoaviakhim, created the Ready for Labor and Defense Test as a competition between the different clubs. The competition promoted health and physical development through fitness which in turn was preparation for labor activities and defense of the Motherland. A series of seven semi-militarized decathlons included such sports as sprinting, cross-country running, swimming, gymnastics, skiing or bike riding (depending on the region), hand grenade throwing, map reading, and rifle target shooting. Silver and gold colored badges were awarded to the highest ranking finishers.

Nearly all of the women pilots we will discuss acquired their flight experience and eventual pilot's licenses from the aforementioned rigorous routines of membership in the Komsomol and/or the Osoaviakhim. In February 1935, the Osoaviakhim had 13 million young men and women members, with 113 flying clubs across the Soviet Union. Within the membership were 600,000 trained sharpshooters, 300,000 qualified parachutists, 50,000 licensed glider pilots, and 500,000 aero-modelers (builders and flyers of model aircraft). The majority of these young men and women went forward into military service even before the threat of war had become apparent.

By 1939, the Osoaviakhim had nearly two million women members alone, the majority of whom had a strong desire to fly aircraft, not just gliders, and were actively pursing a pilot's license. In the early months of 1941, a total of 150 flying clubs existed. One of every three successfully trained pilots from the flying clubs was a young woman.

At the same time, the threat of war in Europe increased on a daily basis. Thousands of young women were trained and ready to fight for their country; they just needed to be allowed to do so.

Author's note: All young members in the aforementioned clubs learned parachuting and glider flying at very young ages. The teaching strategy from these governmental groups was such that parachuting would help the young children overcome a variety of fears. Flying gliders would introduce them to the purest form of flight. Gliders have no engine, no sound, and "glide" on wind currents. The students learned how to maneuver the plane to find the currents, then feel every response from the plane as it slips, slides, and glides along in the air. It is a joy for a young person to experience this form of flight. Those with a passion to fly are immediately hooked and choose to continue on to a powered aircraft and licensure. It is also a win-win situation for the military to have such young men and women trained and ready for service.

Chapter 4

Flight of the Rodina

American Charles Lindbergh made headline news worldwide when he flew his plane, "The Spirit of St. Louis," nonstop across the Atlantic Ocean to Paris in May 1927. "I was astonished at the effect my successful landing in France had on the nations of the world," Lindbergh stated. "To me, it was like a match lighting a bonfire." Indeed, Mr. Lindbergh lit an aviation bonfire worldwide.

History recognizes the period between WWI and WWII as the "Golden Age of Aviation." The slow wood and fabric biplanes utilized in WWI were gradually being replaced in many countries by a variety of sleek metal monoplanes with lightweight, more powerful engines. As the improvements in aircraft progressed, so did the surge of military and civilian interest in aviation. Barnstorming displays of daring aerial feats, air races, long-distance racing, and worldwide competitions to break existing aviation records dominated news stories. Nonmilitary use of aircraft for mail delivery and personal or business travel opened the world to a faster way of life.

One phase in Stalin's plan for rapid industrialization included advancements in aviation. Even before he took leadership of the Soviet Union, plans for improved aviation were seen as a vital and efficient way to transport prisoners to the obscure northern Gulags, transport mail, supplies, and high ranking government officials across the twelve time zones of the vast Union. To Stalin's way of thinking, air transport could increase efficiency and production. However, those obscure Gulag's prisoners and supplies received by air transport were often delayed or cancelled altogether due to the severe winter weather in the northern most regions; trains would then have to slowly make their way to the sites.

After Soviet aviation delegations, along with their top engineers, regularly visited America's most prominent aircraft developers, Boeing, Douglas, Pratt & Whitney, Curtiss-Wright and others, aircraft manufacturing soared to new heights for the Soviets. Between 1928 and 1932 civilian and military aircraft manufacturing plants in the Soviet Union increased in number from 608 to 2,509. Annual aircraft production rose dramatically with over 40,241 planes rolling off assembly lines. Figures released to the media indicate a total of 157,261 aircraft were produced during the Great Patriotic War, of which 125,655 were for military use; 50% were bombers, 39% fighter aircraft, and the remainder were used for reconnaissance or transports.

Construction of airports across the vast country was also increased during this time period. Airports in remote areas were simply cleared strips of grass or dirt while the larger cities had surfaced runways and small terminals.

By 1938, the Soviet Union had the largest air force in the world. The only problem was most of the aircraft were heavy bomber planes best utilized for long distance and record-breaking flights. The Soviet government, Stalin in particular, wanted the world to know they were also game for breaking world aviation records. Media publications would draw world attention to Stalin's technological progress with his industrialization plans. On the home front, Soviet media glorified the nation's record-breaking pilots placing them on proverbial pedestals as role models for youth and symbols of continued progress toward Stalin's socialist utopian dream. To that end, between 1933 and 1938, the Soviet government encouraged, planned, and funded pilots interested in setting and breaking a variety of world aviation records.

In June of 1938 well-known test pilot Vladimir Kokkinake and his navigator, A.M. Bryandinskogo, flew from Moscow to Spassk-Far, a distance of 6,850 miles. Shortly after this famous flight, Stalin wanted Soviet women to undertake a similar record to set an international distance flight by attempting a near straight line flight across the center of the Soviet Union. The end results of both the men and women's record flights would be the opening of air routes from Moscow to Siberia.

Stalin personally selected the three best, most experienced women and provided them with a specially modified aircraft. The plane was an Antonov ANT-37, a long-range medium bomber, which had a modified nose section, upgraded twin radial engines with three blade propellers. At full throttle the engines produced 950 horsepower at 2,250 r.p.m. Maximum speed at sea level was 186 m.p.h. and 212

The ANT-37 long range medium bomber.

m.p.h. at high altitude. All military armament and excess weight not needed for the flight had been removed and larger fuel tanks installed. Landing gear was retracted by electro-hydraulic motors with a mechanical backup. The aircraft was dubbed the "*Rodina,*" a Russian name meaning "Motherland" which seemed an appropriate name for an all woman crew.

The three women chosen by Joseph Stalin were Valentina Grizodubova pilot, Polina Osipenko co-pilot, and Marina Raskova navigator.

Twenty-eight year old pilot Grizodubova was one of the Soviet Union's first woman pilots who had flown since she was fourteen years old. At the time of the Rodina flight she had logged over 5,000 flight hours, held one altitude record, two distance records, and three speed records. She was also an acclaimed concert pianist.

Thirty-one year old co-pilot Osipenko was the daughter of a
Ukrainian farmer who did not favor
her desire to fly. Overcoming many
obstacles, hard work, long hours of
training, and logging many flight
hours she was a celebrated aviatrix
with three altitude records and three
distance records by 1937.

Twenty-six year old navigator
Raskova, a classical trained singer
and musician, was the Soviet Air
Force's first woman navigator.
She taught military navigation for
several years before receiving her
pilot's license in 1935. She also
worked for the Soviet secret police. She had been a navigator on
two previous record setting distance flights, one of which was
with pilot Grizodubova in October 1937.

The original flight date had to be delayed for a short period of time when Marina developed acute appendicitis. To
allow her a full recovery a second flight date was scheduled. All was finally ready as the second date approached.

Grizodubova, Osipenko, and Raskova
publicity photo in front of the Rodina.

The day before the scheduled flight, the three women donned their custom fitted flight suits with heavy fur lined trousers, jackets, and boots, then posed together in front of their plane for the Soviet press photographers and national media. A crowd of dignitaries and government officials asked questions of the women, shook hands and wished them well. The highly anticipated flight of an all-woman crew was publicized around the world, per Stalin's instructions.

Final preparations on the aircraft were completed as the crowd dispersed. Members of the Aeronautic Federation installed three sealed barographs in the fuselage which would provide proof of the flight details in the record setting attempt. The barographs would also be proof that no stops for fuel would have been made after the fuel tanks had been sealed. The problem, realized a bit too late, was the fuel tanks had not been topped off after the engines had been tested and before the tanks were sealed.

On September 24, 1938 the three women climbed aboard the Rodina and took off into overcast skies from Moscow headed for Komsomolsk-on-Amur, a flight distance of just over 3,600 miles, unknowingly, with less than full fuel tanks. They planned to arrive at their destination within twenty-five to thirty hours.

The three women settled in for the long flight as the Rodina quickly gained altitude after her successful departure from the Moscow Metro Aeroport. Marina worked in the glass, bubble-nosed navigation pod (see previous aircraft picture) while Polina and Valentina tended to flight operations in their individual cockpits. Their average speed held steady at around 140 m.p.h. with minimal turbulence.

Marina had three types of navigational aides to work with besides a compass and a sextant: dead-reckoning, when the ground was visible; celestial, using the sun's location during the day or stars at night; and radio signals. Aviation charts of the vast Soviet territories were scarce and conveyed little useful information due to the fact that very few aircraft had traversed the further most eastern regions. As they flew through the daylight hours, the women held their predicted course and maintained radio contact with reporting stations on the ground. The three women communicated with each other via intercom radios. All was uneventful to this point.

As clouds began to thicken and turbulence increased, pilot Grizodubova elected to change altitude, climbing the aircraft in hopes of rising above the approaching storm. This would take a bit more fuel than they had previously calculated. The freezing cold, snowy storm gradually enveloped the plane roughly battering it and pushing it slightly off course. Ice began building up on the wings adding weight to the aircraft and requiring another increase in fuel consumption. The cabin temperatures dropped to a bone chilling -24 degrees. There were no cabin heaters.

They had now been flying over twenty hours and, by their calculations, should have reached their planned destination of Komsomolsk-on-Amur. Visibility was near zero as heavy snow continued to slam at the plane while strong winds pushed them even more off course. The radio-to-ground communication was not working; it may have frozen in the sub-zero cabin temperature or they might have been over an isolated region where no radio communications existed. The women were now disoriented and lost. They were also angry that the well-planned high-profile record flight by an all woman crew was being scuttled by an unpredicted snow storm.

Raskova suggested to Grizodubova they drop in altitude so she might get a better sense of their location. At nearly 7,000 feet Raskova spotted the Sea of Okhotsk below them and strongly urged Grizodubova to immediately change course to a westerly heading, back from where they had just come. Grizodubova dutifully turned the aircraft around.

Just as the aircraft made it back over land the low fuel alarm light began flashing. The alarm indicated only thirty minutes of fuel remained. Below them Marina could make out tall trees and small open patches. The women had no time to search for a safe place to land, and a crash landing was imminent. Since the navigation pod was a plexiglass bubble and would likely be the first destroyed in a crash, Grizodubova ordered Raskova to bail out. Time was running out for an escape as the fuel alarm was now flashing furiously.

Marina quickly tightened the straps of her parachute, secured her pistol and made her way to the emergency hatch. As the plane dropped to an altitude of 6,500 feet, she leaped out into the freezing air, pulled her ripcord when she cleared the plane then watched the Rodina as it flew on and slowly dropped in altitude. As she floated lazily down to solid ground, the air was silent and still. The only thing she could hear was the sound of Rodina's big radial engines sputtering as the last drops of fuel were consumed carrying the plane further and further away from her. She made a mental note of the direction the plane was headed so she could make her way toward it for rescue. Once it was out of sight, she concentrated on the ground below. All she saw was a thick forest of tall trees and thought it would be a difficult landing at best. Her brain quickly searched for previous training tips on how to survive a parachute-landing in a tree, but she could only come up with how to prepare for a haphazard landing; alas, she just hoped for the best.

The pilot and co-pilot continued their descent while the fuel indicators dropped to zero and the engines completely sputtered out. Together they spotted an open area, free of trees and braced for a hard landing. Pilot Grizodubova did not deploy the landing gear for fear of catapulting the plane, instead she chose a wheels up, belly landing. The ground was frozen swamp which made for an unbelievably perfect landing with very little damage to the Rodina - a true test of any pilot's skill. The two women climbed out of the plane unscathed and waited. Even though they had been unable to send any type of emergency call for help, they assumed rescue teams would begin a search after the plane failed to arrive at its planned destination. The Rodina would provide them shelter from the freezing cold and a minimal food supply until help arrived. They would also stay near the plane in hopes that Marina would soon find them. They knew their location was somewhere in the far eastern region of Siberia. It was later pinpointed by rescuers that they had landed on the taiga near the head of the Amgun River close to the remote village of Kerbi which sat on the banks of the Amur River where it joined the Amgun.

Meanwhile, Marina did not become entangled in a tall pine tree as she had feared, but the hard landing on frozen ground severely injured her legs. She gathered her parachute and began a slow, painful walk/limp/crawl in the direction she had seen the Rodina disappear from view. The going was rough and extremely cold. The forest was thick and dark with trees and brush as well as startled animals.

She was dismayed to find, in her haste to jump from the plane, she had forgotten her emergency kit. All she had for survival were a couple of chocolate bars and some mints in her flight suit pocket. The forest was full of frozen edible mushrooms, berries and birch leaves as well as water from small streams. She took advantage of the food sources when she found them then curled up in her parachute to rest her painful legs and tried to keep warm. Marina trudged on and on and on. For ten long painful days she stayed on course of tracking down the Rodina and her two fellow crew members.

When the plane failed to reach its planned destination, a massive search by land and air was initiated over the eastern region which covered nearly two million square kilometers. Sadly, two rescue planes collided midair and killed sixteen searchers, one of whom was a high-ranking Red Air Force official. This information was not released to the media at the time of the incident and only surfaced many years later.

Eight days after the Rodina's flight ended unceremoniously, a couple of villagers found the plane and notified the authorities of its location. Rescuers were then flown to the site and deployed a parachute team, which landed near the wreckage. They were equipped with food, medical supplies and the directional knowledge of how to get to the nearby river for transport out of the area. Marina had seen the rescue planes flying overhead followed by the parachute team and knew she was getting closer to the downed plane. She trudged on hungry, thirsty, and in terrible pain, but hopeful.

Two days after the Rodina was located by the rescue team, Marina finally reached the plane exhausted and barely able to walk due to her injured legs, but in good spirits. She was carried to the river by stretcher while the rest of the group walked. Collapsible canoes carried all of them down the river to a nearby village where they awaited further transport.

Reports of the daring rescue efforts began appearing in the daily *Pravda* newspaper only after the plane had been spotted (no news reports, by order of the government, had been printed earlier when the plane had gone missing). The biggest attention getting articles related to Raskova's ten day ordeal traipsing through the forest, severely injured, without food and still managed to find the plane and her fellow crew. She was highly praised as a hero by the entire nation.

The trip back to Moscow took several weeks by train. At each stop along the way, the women were greeted as heroes by tens of thousands of well-wishers. At the Belorussia Railway Station they were met by Nikita Khrushchev (secretary of the Central Committee of the Ukraine at that time) then shuttled off to a parade which took them to the Kremlin where Stalin was anxiously awaited their arrival.

Stalin was elated and reportedly greeted each woman "with kisses and a hearty hug." The Rodina had flown 3,672 miles in 26 hours and 29 minutes setting a new

Osipenko   Raskova   Grizodubova

record for an all-woman flight crew. Worldwide media was notified. Celebrations and honors began immediately, all under the direction of Stalin. During a long state dinner honoring the women, Stalin spoke of the ancient times of matriarchy in the Soviet Union. He concluded his speech by toasting the women, "Today these three women have avenged the heavy centuries of the oppression of women."

All three women were recognized and decorated with the Hero of the Soviet Union (HSU) award, the first women to be so honored prior to the Great Patriotic War. Each had a postage stamp struck in her honor and each received a financial reward of 25,000 rubles ($351.89 in today's U.S. currency) for their "loyal service to the Soviet ideal." Two Soviet authors, Lazar Frontman and Lev Khvat were commissioned to write *The Heroic Flight of the Rodina,* which was hurriedly published by the end of 1938.

Stalin publicly added his boastful congratulations to the world by pointing out the Soviet women had established a record of non-stop flight longer than Charles Lindbergh's flight across the Atlantic—Lindbergh flew 3,610 miles in thirty-three and one-half hours while the Soviet women flew 3,671.44 miles in twenty-six hours, twenty-nine minutes—not much of a difference but he capitalized on it anyway!

Typical of Soviet leadership and propaganda of the time, very few words were mentioned about the "crash" landing. A heavily retouched aerial photo of the Rodina was later published and described as "the landing site" of the record setting flight.

Author's note: Conflicting sources say the plane was heavily damaged and dismantled by scavenging villagers. Other sources say the plane was relatively unscathed and remained at the crash site until the early 1990s. Due to the difficult terrain it was not feasible to remove it or attempt to fly it out. It is not clear from any available source what the eventual outcome for the aircraft was.

At a later gala honoring the women, Commissar of Heavy Industry, Lazar Kaganovich, remarked that if the Soviet Union is ever attacked, "We have flyers who can chase the enemy back to his own territory." Unknown by most at that time the war clouds were quickly gathering across Europe. His words would become prophetic in just a couple of years.

As the celebrations winded down, Stalin stepped forward to announce the end of the government sponsored quests for record setting/breaking aviation fetes. A male aviator had been killed a few weeks prior to the announcement trying to break a flight record, much to Stalin's dismay. He announced, "The government will be extremely severe henceforth toward permitting record-setting flights. The lives of the pilots are more precious to us than any records, no matter how great or renowned they may be."

Even so, by 1939 Soviet women pilots had captured more aviation records than women in any other country, including the U.S.A. Soviet airwomen accounted for nearly one-third of all the pilots trained in the U.S.S.R. at that time.

The flight of the Rodina marked an important turning point in the Soviet Union's history of women's aviation. Grizodubova and Raskova were idolized by young and old alike. They were an inspiration to young girls and women across the Soviet Union. Raskova's book, *Zapiski Shturmana, Notes of a Navigator,* quickly became the motivation for thousands of them to learn to fly. Grizodubova and Raskova were both deluged with notes and letters from school girls asking what they should do to become pilots, or how to gain entry into flying schools. Grizodubova was not a very personable sort, she took care of business in a rather brusk manner and did not like to be bothered. Raskova was kind, caring and enjoyed helping others experience the joy of flying. She personally answered thousands of letters encouraging each to pursue their dreams of flight.

Sadly, co-pilot Polina Osipenko was killed in an air crash in May 1939, just eight months after the famed Rodina flight. She was given a public funeral in Red Square with Stalin himself as one of the pallbearers. Her ashes were inurned in the Kremlin Wall, a place of honor for National heroes.

The importance of the Rodina flight with the idolization of Marina Raskova sets the stage for the Night Witches story. But first, we will jump ahead sixty years for an additional story acknowledging the importance of that flight and how it has been recognized and remembered as a worldwide turning point in women's aviation history. Read on!

Chapter 5

The Bridge of Wings Flight

The flight of the Rodina was newsworthy around the world. Aviation history books featured the story under the headings of Women Aviation Pioneers. In America, the story of Grizodubova, Osipenko and Raskova's amazing flight of courage and stamina ranked just as high as the record setting flights of Lindbergh and Earhart.

Sixty years later, a group of women decided to recreate the Rodina flight across Russia as a reminder of the stories, lost or forgotten, in the textbooks of women's aviation history.

Two American pilots, Nikki Mitchell and Rhonda Miles, began plans for an around-the-world flight to include a

Nikki Mitchell (L) Rhonda Miles (R)

commemorative flight with Russian pilots Khalide Makagonova (1984 Women's World Aerobatic Champion) and Natalia Vinokourova (commercial pilot for Russian Magadan Air) to recreate the Rodina flight. The adventurous plan was dubbed the Bridge of Wings Flight.

On July 4, 1998, after two years of planning, fund raising, miles of red tape, and permits from Russian officials (the last of which was received three days before the scheduled flight), the two American women climbed aboard Mary Beth, their fully equipped Maule M-5, single engine, tail dragger airplane, and departed Nashville, Tennessee headed for Moscow, Russia. Their flight path took them North to West Virginia, New York, Maine, Canada then on to Newfoundland, Greenland, Iceland, Scotland, Norway, Sweden, Finland, St. Petersburg, Russia and finally arriving at the Tushino Airdrome in Moscow, Russia July 23.

The Maule M-5 lovingly
called Mary Beth.

They were greeted by a crowd of television cameras, reporters, locals bearing flowers, singing and dancing in their native costumes. The two American women were also greeted by a club of women aviators known as Aviatrissa, as well as Khalide and Natalia who would be making the commemorative flight along with them. Galina Korchuganova, the 1960 World Champion in Aerobatic Flying and a test pilot at the time, stepped forward and warmly greeted the gathering. Galina was the President of Aviatrissa then and was called upon to present the following:

"The club of women aviators, Aviatrissa, which includes famous aviatrixes from Russia and Former Soviet Republics (now independent states) with great enthusiasm greet the intentions of the American pilots Nikki Mitchell and Rhonda Miles as they retrace the route of the Russian plane Rodina, in July 1998 to commemorate the 60th anniversary of the flight by the Russian aviatrixes Valentina Grizodubova, Paulina Ossipenko, and Marina Raskova.

We are ready to render any possible assistance and participation with this flight. We ask everybody who can to promote this important initiative and support financially these American women aviators.

We are sure this joint event will be of great importance for further mutual understanding and strengthening friendships between the peoples of our countries."

The American and Russian pilots met the next day with the project organizers and finalized flight details. The Russian air traffic controllers had scheduled a nationwide strike but upon hearing of the planned flight rescheduled the strike until after the Americans had cleared Russian airspace. There was also a problem with obtaining enough aviation fuel for the long flight. Avgas is not very plentiful in Russia. The Russian government came to the rescue by flying fuel via military plane to many of the stops the women would be making along the route. Unlike the original Rodina flight, the Bridge of Wings flight would be making fueling and rest stops along the way.

The two aircraft ready for their Commemorative Flight,
Mary Beth and the Russian An-2.

The Russians insisted the Americans have navigators and translators aboard their aircraft. This obstacle was easily overcome by having Russian pilot Natalia fly with American pilot Nikki in the Russian An-2 plane, while American Rhonda would fly with Russian Khalide in the Mary Beth. They would fly in side-by-side formation with a Russian military crew following in another An-2 plane.

After the meeting, Nikki and Rhonda, along with their entourage, visited the famed resting sites of Grizodubova, Osipenko and Raskova in Red Square. Next was a special welcoming from nearly fifty former WWII fighter pilots, the famed Night Witches. Each proudly displayed an array of well-earned and treasured medals, ribbons and awards that adorned their suits or dresses. The Night Witches each greeted the American pilots proudly through their translators.

Finally, July 27, 1998 the day of departure for the Rodina Commemorative Flight had arrived! The press was out in force begging for interviews, snapping pictures or video taping the preflight pilot routines, while well wishers with bundles of flowers happily greeted the pilots. Suddenly, a Russian official hurried out to the women to anxiously and apologetically inform them they must have a Russian medical exam completed before they could takeoff. "Not to worry, the doctor is coming!" he nervously assured them as he swept his gaze across the area while wringing his hands; a trickle of sweat rolled down his cheek. Their scheduled departure was in twenty minutes!

Within minutes a very old, red Fiat came careening across the field screeching to a halt next to the planes. A very large woman sat in the backseat. The doctor had arrived! She motioned for Nikki to enter her office exam room in the backseat where she checked her pulse, asked her if she knew her blood pressure, "is it high or low?" Then asked if she felt fine. Next Rhonda had the same extensive exam in the cramped exam room. The medical forms were then stamped, papers were signed, handed out the window, engine revved a few times, smoke billowed from the exhaust, then the little red Fiat peeled and squealed off the runway. Nikki and Rhonda looked at each other in disbelief and chuckled as they watched the little red car disappear in a cloud of smoke. If only all flight exams back home could be that easy, they thought!

An old Russian military fuel truck chugged up to both planes and began filling the tanks of the An-2. When the attendant tried to fit the nozzle into the tank of the Mary Beth, it didn't fit; it was too large. With a big smile aimed at the American pilots, the fueler pushed the nozzle over the tank opening and began transferring the Avgas into the aircraft tank. Since there was a large gap at the fitting, fuel began squirting and spraying out onto the wing.

Rhonda and Khalide were under the wing where the fueling was taking place and were subsequently sprayed with the Avgas. There was no time to shower and change clothes so the two women climbed aboard the plane and prepared for takeoff. How do you say "stinky" in Russian?

For the most part, the flights went well with few or minor difficulties. At each stop the pilots were greeted by cheering crowds, dignitaries, bands, native costumes and dancers. Some of the stops had elders who were alive when the actual history-making flight had taken place and were thrilled to greet the four women pilots.

They flew over desolate, sparsely inhabited areas, tiny villages, larger cities, swamps, mountains, and glaciers. On August 5, 1998 they reached Osipenko, the end of the Commemorative Flight. As both aircraft passed over the Rodina crash site, they dropped flowers from each aircraft then landed at the nearby airfield.

After a brief rest at the town's hotel, the group was taken to a nearby monument honoring the Flight of the Rodina then on to the museum dedicated to the three Rodina women. At the museum they were honored to meet the daughter-in-law of one of the men who had found the Rodina shortly after it had crashed and notified authorities of their location.

Next, on to the town hall for another gathering of local townspeople singing and dancing in their native costumes, followed by a question and answer session. The American pilots were in awe of the special tributes paid the original Rodina women at the same time the Russian people were in awe of the American women paying tribute and acknowledging the significance of their aviation heroes. It was definitely a win-win event for everyone.

Bridge of Wings pilots, l to r: Khalide, Nikki, Rhonda, Natalia.

Nikki and Rhonda headed for home flying Mary Beth via the Northern route crossing the Bering Sea, Alaska, Canada, Washington, Montana, Iowa, Missouri, and back to the starting point of Nashville, Tennessee. The trip took a total of forty-nine days from beginning to end with a total of fifty-three landings. The FAA (Federal Aviation Administration) presented the two with the Top Flight Award for outstanding contributions to General Aviation and the Ambassadors For Aviation Award in recognition of their memorable flight; the flight truly became a Bridge of Wings between the United States and Russia.

The historic flight of the Rodina and successes of women in aviation were once again recalled.

Now we will flip back sixty years and continue on with finding the Night Witches!

Chapter 6

Marina Raskova

Although it took several months for her injured legs to heal after Raskova's famed flight in the Rodina, she did not slip off quietly or maintain a low profile. Quite the opposite! Raskova was a household name across the Soviet Union, even to the peasants in the farthest outlying regions. The British had pilot Amy Johnson, America had aviator Amelia Earhart, and the Soviets had their beloved Marina Raskova. As the clouds of war approached, two American women, Jacqueline Cochran and Nancy Love, were key figures in the organization and implementation of the Women's Air Service Pilots (WASP) at the same time Soviet pilots had Marina Raskova organizing three women's aviation fighter regiments.

Marina Mikhailovna Malinina was born March 28, 1912 in Moscow. She was a very beautiful child with big blue eyes and long, silky black hair. Her father was an opera singer and music instructor while her mother was a teacher. Her brother, Boris, was a scientist. Tragically, her beloved father was killed after being struck by a motorcycle when Marina was just seven years old.

Marina had early aspirations of becoming an opera singer or a concert pianist. At the age of six she attended the Pushkin School of Music. She was accepted into a conservatory at the age of ten then transferred to a technical school of music. While in high school Marina suffered a severe middle ear infection that caused a slight loss of hearing. That changed her course of studies from music to chemistry. She also studied French and Italian, became fluent in both, which garnered her high marks. After graduation in 1929 she began work in a dye factory as a chemist. She met and married Sergey Raskova, an engineer, then gave birth to their daughter Tanya in 1930. Unfortunately, they divorced in 1935; however, Marina retained her married name, Raskova.

In 1931, at the age of nineteen, Marina was hired as a draftswoman in the Aero Navigation Laboratory at the Air Force Academy where she learned of the many opportunities aviation had to offer besides glider piloting. She began studies in navigation then passed the aviation navigator exam in 1934 to become the first female navigator in the Soviet Air Force. At age twenty-two she became the first female navigation instructor to male officers at the Nikolai Zhukovskii Air Academy. The men were skeptical of her knowledge and abilities at first but were quickly impressed by her knowledge, teaching skills, and abilities.

In 1935 she received her pilot's license and began teaching instrument flight and advanced navigation to command personnel. She quickly discovered a preference to navigate rather than to pilot an aircraft. Her navigation skills were well known in aviation circles and she was called upon to participate in several record setting flights. In October 1937, Marina and Valentina Grizodubova established a women's long distance, non-stop flight of 898 miles. In 1938, at the age of twenty-six, she participated in three more record flights, one covering 1,087 miles, another at 1,392 miles and the Rodina flight, previously detailed.

When the Germans invaded the Soviet Union on June 22, 1941, there were only a handful of women serving as military pilots. However, there were thousands of young women who had been trained in military ways and held pilot certifications from Osoaviakhim air clubs. Many of the women did not hesitate to immediately volunteer. Their applications for pilot services were promptly denied, delayed or dropped altogether. At that time, the military only accepted applications for nurses, sharpshooters, antiaircraft gunners, or communications operators. According to officials, the reason for the denials was that high houred women pilots were needed as instructors at the flying schools in order for the male instructors to go to the front lines.

Although there were conflicting documents and articles about how the all-women's military aviation groups were formed, it was generally accepted and acknowledged that Marina Raskova, then a Major in the Soviet Air Force, played a pivotal role. Due to her previous aviation accomplishments, her leadership skills, her close connections to

Joseph Stalin as well as her position on the People's Defense Committee, she was a force to be reckoned with in organizing such a group of women. Just before Stalin, along with his military officials, gave her the final go-ahead to form combat regiments composed of women, Marina announced to all interested female pilots the call to service over Radio Moscow. The print version appeared in the *Pravda* newspaper the next day. Her speech in part stated,

"...the Soviet woman - she is the hundreds of thousands of drivers, tractor operators, and pilots, who are ready at any moment to sit down in a combat machine and plunge into battle...Dear sisters! The hour has come for harsh retribution! Stand in the ranks of the warriors for freedom...!"

On October 8, 1941, Marina received the official Order Number 0099 from the People's Commissariat of Defense which directed the formation of three women's aviation regiments by the first of December. The three new regiments of Aviation Group 122 were to consist of a fighter unit, a dive-bomber unit, and a night-bomber unit.

To form her staff, Raskova gathered together a small group of women who were then serving in the military. They immediately began to make preparations and plans as to how best to proceed in recruiting women for the three regiments.

In response to her radio and newspaper calls to service, an avalanche of applications and requests were received within a matter of days. Thousands of interviews began, not only for pilots but also for mechanics, engineers and support staff - all women. Komsomol and Osoaviakhim groups carefully screened their members who wanted to volunteer for aviation and non-aviation positions. Those with the highest marks and deemed worthy were sent directly to Raskova. Due to the rigid guidelines for physical fitness set by the two groups, those volunteers chosen from them by Raskova were not required to undergo any sort of medical or agility testing.

Pilots with documented high flight hours were quickly accepted by Raskova herself. Those with a minimum of five-hundred hours would likely become fighter and bomber pilots. Those with lower flight hours were considered as well but would be utilized as navigators, backup pilots or machine gunners.

With nearly 2,000 women volunteers selected in just a matter of days, training preparations were finally ready to begin. The volunteers would not receive a military ranking until after their extensive training was accomplished and before their assignment to one of the three regiments.

On October 17, Aviation Group 122 boarded trains in Moscow for the long journey to the town of Engels on the Volga River. Before training began and after the volunteers had been sworn in to service, Marina greeted her group with a rousing speech:

"History remembers those women who participated in battles. But all of these women were individuals, and they

fought in men's units. Such were conditions then. We are Soviet women, women of a free socialist nation. In our Constitution it is written that women have equal rights in all fields of activity. Today you took the military oath, you vowed to faithfully defend the homeland. So let's vow once more, together, to stand to our last breath in defense of our beloved homeland. Study persistently, with perseverance! The examination will be given on the field of battle."

Chapter 7

Preparations Begin

Nearly all of Raskova's volunteer recruits reported to Moscow on October 17, 1941 where they boarded railcars to begin their journey to Engels for training. Although it was only October, the outside air temperature was four degrees below zero. Fortunately, the railcars were heated troop carriers but not everyone was warm and cozy. The journey was a five hundred mile, nine day trip with many stops along the way.

At the same time, tens of thousands of Moscow's citizens were fleeing the advancing Germans with thousands taking any available space on the trains. Military troops had first priority which left little space for those fleeing the city. Nonetheless, the train stopped at every station where massive movements of people got on or off. There were no dining cars, no food, water or toilet facilities available on the packed trains. At some of the stations, a few of the volunteer recruits would rush off the train and purchase bread, fruit or milk then share with fellow recruits.

The journey was long and difficult, but the train finally pulled into the Engels station. Nearly two thousand weary young women gathered on the train platform in the pitch dark of night, surrounded by an eerie cold, misty fog and no one to greet them. Marina quickly arranged for transport to the school. After what seemed like hours waiting in the dark and cold, several troop transport trucks noisily lumbered up to the station. The tired, hungry young women piled in for a bumpy, uncomfortable ride to the school several miles from the station.

Engels Flying School had been the site of aviation training since the early 1930s where thousands of pilots received the standard three year flight course. With the Germans hell bent on taking the Soviet Union, this out-of-the-way training base became a small city focused on just one thing: training pilots as fast as they could. During the war years, a total of fourteen regiments trained at Engels were sent to the front lines, including Raskova's three.

The base was not just for Raskova's regiments at that the time, it was also where the men received their military flight training. When the women arrived, a dark cloud of commotion and distrust rolled quickly across the base. The men jeered at them, called them degrading names, "the skirts regiment," mocked them, and did all they could to dissuade them from their volunteer call-to-duty. The majority of disrespectful men had been drafted so were likely a bit resentful of all these women who had volunteered. The disrespect only encouraged the girls to push themselves as hard as they could, both physically and mentally, to outperform their male counterparts and prove their worth.

Since the women's regiment received no special or differential treatment from the men, upon their arrival they were sent to the barbershop for a military haircut, a buzz cut; hair had to be no longer than two inches all over the head. To differentiate them from the men, the barber had been instructed to leave one long lock of hair hanging down the front side of the face. A Soviet woman's pride and joy was her hair. Most young women had never cut their hair. It was worn in long braids and wrapped around the head or allowed to hang freely, often reaching below the waist. Long thick braids and beautiful colorful curls fell to the floor as the women cried in horror. Several days shortly thereafter during a surprise visit, a high ranking official was stunned to find the women looking like men with their military haircuts and rescinded the order. No further buzz cuts for new women recruits, but it would take months and months for those already shorn to regrow their beautiful hair.

Next, they were issued uniforms. Men's uniforms. Shirts, jackets, underwear, as well as thick-soled boots from England called "Churchills." Pilots received a sheepskin lined flight jacket, padded leather helmet and flight goggles, all way oversized. The men's underwear was so large it fell to the floor when pulled on. The trousers were longer than some women were tall. The boots were so large the women could turn their feet completely around in the opposite direction which made walking and marching nearly impossible. They were not issued socks, instead they were given *portyanki*, foot cloths or wraps, which were triangular or square pieces of fabric—flannel for winter, cotton for summer—that were to be securely wrapped around the feet to prevent chafing in the boots. The women thought that was a joke since their feet didn't even touch the insides of the boot!

Many of the women who were handy with needle, thread, and scissors quickly found their skills put to use. Strips of cloth were cut from the underwear, shirts, jackets, and trousers. The garment was sized to fit and hand sewn, the scrap cloth put to use in the boots. First the boots were stuffed with straw then the cloth strips were layered over the straw; more straw for a tighter fit and cloth for comfort. In just a short period of time, the women had uniforms that fit and were somewhat comfortable; however, the boots remained a problem for some time. The men took notice and soon began shyly asking the women to also alter their ill-fitting uniforms.

Three meals a day were prepared for all the students on the base. Food was becoming scarce across the nation, especially meat. The government procured harvested foodstuffs from the collective farms to feed the military first. Three meals a day for the majority of those at Engels was considered a luxury since many had come from homes and families only able to share one small meal a day, if that.

The training was extremely intensive, mentally and physically exacting and psychologically demanding. The flight techniques and navigation courses alone usually took eighteen to thirty-six months to complete. The women now had six months to complete those same studies. Students studied twelve to fourteen hours a day either in classrooms, or within their chosen fields, i.e. mechanics, armorers, gunnery, etc. Raskova supervised all aspects of training often studying along with them as well as taking the same exams. She constantly challenged herself on tactical ideas to pass along to her recruits.

There were few, if any, textbooks. Those that were available were seriously outdated and worn from use. During the early war years there was a severe shortage of paper for textbooks and writing paper. Only the newspaper and government offices were allowed to have fresh blank paper. Old newspapers were used for note taking with students writing between the lines and in the wide margins of the paper.

In addition to the long days and nights studying, both men and women recruits were also called upon to assist in harvesting crops on nearby collective farms before winter set in. To some of the recruits it was a refreshing change to get outdoors while others only viewed the work as time away from studying.

Since the majority of Raskova's girls were already trained pilots, they focused on more intense studies of meteorology, aviation principles, aerodynamics, and map reading. They were also taught how to read intelligence reports including how to look for any newly reported enemy fighter tactics and how to detect troop movements. Flashcards were used to help memorize the identity of enemy aircraft using multiple silhouette views.

Pilots were taught the finer points of flying the aircraft while navigators were taught to direct the pilots to the target, aim and drop the bombs, then return to the home base airfield. Combat flying techniques, bombing, dive bombing, and aircraft gunnery had to be mastered. These techniques were taught utilizing the principles of the "three layers of warring aircraft over a vertical battlefield." The lowest layers were the ground attack bombers, the second layers were the fighters destroying the enemy bombers, and the third layers were the fighters protecting their own bombers. The importance of this training would determine which pilots would be best suited and assigned to the three distinct regiments soon to be created.

Mockups of German tanks, planes, railcars, motor cars, and cannons were set up for bombing and machine gun practice on a nearby designated bombing range. Targets were also set up on the ground for pistol shooting practice. Every pilot, as well as some navigators, would be given an automatic pistol. The pistol was to be holstered on their person

Soviet pistol similar to what pilots carried.

prior to every flight for self-defense in case they were shot down behind enemy lines. Marksmanship was graded as well as the ability to take the weapon apart, clean it and put it back together correctly, in a timely manner.

Marina rarely took a break oftentimes working deep into the night. On more than one occasion, she was found sound asleep at her desk surrounded by stacks of paper or lying on a nearby cot fully clothed in her uniform and boots. When or if she took a break, one might have found her at a piano playing Brahms or Schubert compositions or accompanying several of her recruits who loved to sing.

Spirits were lifted beyond measure on November 7, 1941 when Marina's volunteers took the military oath. Studying and training continued in earnest. Small delicate girls were becoming strong courageous fighter pilots, navigators, mechanics, armorers, and crew. Marina told the girls, "...you can do anything. Nothing is impossible. If we want to accomplish something, we can manage it ourselves."

The harsh winter weather of 1941 at Engles was the worst on record, but many of the girls were used to dealing with the Soviet Union's freezing, snowy weather. However, they were not used to dealing with the extreme cold when aircraft were involved. With temperatures reaching thirty-five degrees below zero the women quickly learned not to touch any metal with bare hands. Skin would stick to the metal which resulted in serious injuries and bloody, skinless hands. Armorers had the hardest time learning how to arm and rack the bombs using heavy gloves but figured it out quickly after their hands stuck to a bomb just one time.

Mechanics who had to haul compressed air cylinders to the aircraft, heavy metal ammunition cans and more, also suffered in the extreme weather. They also had to maintain the aircraft which seemed to need constant, daily repairs. There were no warm hangars from which the women worked. They did their jobs outside in the freezing temperatures of winter or the blistering heat of summer.

Pilots and navigators wore heavy sheepskin lined flight jackets over their flight suits in the extreme cold. They also

Ready for winter flight.

had heavy gloves to wear during flights in their open cockpit planes but found it difficult to handle maps and instruments with the big clumsy gloves. Padded leather helmets with ear flaps were somewhat sufficient in protecting the head and ears from the cold. Goggles might have sheepskin around the inside to prevent them from sticking to the skin but were in short supply. Some of the pilots cut pieces of cloth or sheepskin and lined their own goggles for comfort and nonstick.

Frost bite, sunburn, extreme fatigue, and anxiety were common. Colds, flu, pneumonia, and skin infections were also recurring problems due to the extreme cold. These difficulties with weather were not just confined to training at Engels but also persisted throughout the war in many of their home base locations.

The young women also learned to deal with death at Engels. One of the first regimental loss of lives occurred on March 10, 1942 when three planes took off on a nighttime training mission headed for the bombing range. A snow storm had been escalating which decreased visibility and increased disorientation. At the bombing range, burning torches were quickly lit around the perimeter to help pilots and their navigators reorient themselves. Torches were also lit back at the base to help them find their way back.

The training assignment that night was for three planes with pilot and navigator onboard to launch about one to two minutes apart. The lead plane would fly to the bomb drop zone, release her bombs, fly away from the lit area into the dark, make a turn, and fly back to the airfield. The second and third plane would do the same, maintaining the one to two minute interval between them. The first pilot was successful in dropping her bombs and returning to base. As the snowfall became heavier, the second and third pilots became disoriented in the combination of dark and snow; they could not differentiate up from down and could not see the torches. They had no instrumentation to assist them in determining a horizon. Both planes crashed to the ground from an estimated altitude of 2,000 feet instantly killing all four.

The regiment was devastated. All the girls had become close, forming a tight-knit unit. Many had never experienced the loss of a fellow friend. When Marina came upon the group of sobbing, grieving girls she gathered them together to comfort and encourage them by saying, "My dar-lings, my girls, squeeze your heart, stop crying, you shouldn't be sobbing, because in the future you have to face so many of them that you will ruin yourselves com-pletely." Marina's words would become prophetic as those that heard them would recall them when they learned the news of Marina's own death a short time later.

Marina watched her recruits very carefully as they com-pleted their studies and demonstrations before making her final decisions as to who would go where and why. After all, her reputation was on the line to prove her idea correct that women regiments would be valuable assets in the war effort. At the end of the six months, enough women quali-fied for assignments in one of the three different regiments. Few failed to complete the training or dropped out for any reason.

Initially, each regiment would have three squadrons of ten to twenty aircraft, thirteen or more pilots and navigators for those aircraft, a large group of mechanics, armament fitters, and support crew for a total of over 400 women in each regiment. The remainder of volunteers would be as-signed as backup in all positions.

Meanwhile, the Germans were carrying out Hitler's or-ders to annihilate the Soviets. Villages were overtaken and burned to the ground, crops were pillaged then burned, farm animals butchered, food stores taken. Soviet soldiers and citizens were killed, captured, or sent to German prison camps by the tens of thousands daily.

The Soviet nation was faltering rapidly.

Chapter 8

The 586th and the 587th

Marina posted her choices for the three regiments based on the pilot's flight hours and their successes during training. All were ready and eager to take their places and begin what they had trained for. The three regiments were each numbered in the "500" series indicating they were of special interest to the GKO (the State Committee for Defense). The regiments, as well as Marina Raskova, were to be carefully scrutinized. After all, they were to become the world's first women's combat aviation units and Stalin would not be humiliated.

The 586th Fighter Aviation Regiment
The first regiment to leave Engels was the 586th on April 16, 1942. The defensive fighter regiment was assigned to active service at Saratov, near Stalingrad with Major Tamara Kazarinova in Command. This unit was often paired with men's regiments and utilized men as mechanics because women had not yet received enough aircraft mechanic training on Yak fighter planes at Engels. Together they were tasked with protecting fixed Soviet targets (military installations, factories, communication and transportation lines, etc.) from enemy attacks during daylight hours. They would also provide air cover for advancing Soviet ground troops.

Many of the recruits selected for the regiment were high houred pilots, instructors, or civil aviation pilots. Three members of the regiment, Raisa Beliaeva, Evgeniia Prokhorova, and Valeriia Khomiakova, were well-known aerobatic team pilots who flew in Soviet airshows prior to the war.

Pilot Raisa Beliaeva was often called upon to fly high-profile missions or escort Soviet officials including Nikita Khrushchev, now the political officer for the Stalingrad front at that time, and Air Defense Forces Commander Major-General Gromadin. Raisa was later killed in a plane crash thought to be caused by a mysterious, unknown aircraft malfunction.

Pilot Evgeniia Prokhorova held several world records prior to the war. During a fighter escort she was forced to crash land after being engulfed in a heavy, unexpected snowstorm. She was found the next day, frozen to death, trapped in her overturned plane.

Pilot Valeriia Khomiakova was recognized as the first woman in the world to shoot down an enemy aircraft at night. Shortly after being recognized and awarded for this fete in Moscow, she returned to her home base exhausted from the festivities and lengthy trip. Her Commander, Major Kazarinova allowed her no rest period upon her return, instead, ordered her to immediately suit-up and take off on a mission. Valeriia was killed when her plane crashed on takeoff. The circumstances of the order and resultant crash raised serious questions about the leadership capabilities of the Major. After Major Kazarinova had served as Commander for six months, many of the pilots complained of her poor judgement and inability to instill a sense of teamwork within the regiment. Those voicing concerns to her, or about her, received hazardous assignments which usually caused accidents or some type of serious problem including deaths, such as the mysterious cause of Raisa's crash.

Kazarinova was not well liked or trusted by a majority of the regiment members, men or women. Trust issues surfaced when several complained the Major did not pilot an aircraft herself supposedly due to a previous leg injury which caused her to limp. The thought was that not being an active pilot would lead to the inability to make educated decisions regarding flight assignments to current pilots.

Marina Raskova was disappointed to hear of the multiple problems, accidents, and deaths within the 586th, but she did not want to jeopardize her ongoing efforts to organize the other two regiments. She worked quickly and quietly to resolve the main problem which was obviously Major Kazarinova.

Major Kazarinova's command of the 586th ended shortly after the death of pilot Khomiakova. She was abruptly dismissed and replaced by Major Aleksandr Gridnev. His appointment was met with misgivings by the women pilots, but he quickly proved to be fair and trustworthy.

Under his command, two women from the regiment, Raisa Surnachevskaia and Tamara Pamiatnykh, saved a troop train packed with allied troops from England passing through the rail junction at Kastornaia en route to the Battle of Kursk. The two pilots each engaged forty-two German bombers, shot down four and caused enough damage to multiple aircraft to prevent any bombs from being dropped on the troop train. The two women were recognized and rewarded with inscribed gold watches by King George VI of England however, they received no recognition by their own Soviet officials. That was somewhat unusual and was later questioned by Gridney and Raskova.

Yak fighter plane

The 586th Fighter Aviation Regiment pilots flew Yak aircraft for 4,419 combat sorties (missions), destroyed thirty-eight enemy aircraft, damaged forty-two in one hundred - twenty-five air engagements. Squadron Commander Olga Yamshchikova flew ninety-three sorties while Lieutenant Maria Kuznetsova flew over two hundred-four sorties. Unfortunately, none of the regiment pilots received a single Hero of the Soviet Union award nor did the regiment receive the prestigious status of Guards.

Author's note: The Soviet Guards designation was introduced in September 1941, just after the Great Patriotic War began, in accordance and by order of the People's Commissar of Defense. The award was ceremoniously presented to military units after demonstrating or distinguishing themselves as elite in their exemplary performance during a specific battle or campaign. Once recognized, the unit often received better equipment, clothing, and supplies. Each unit received a special flag denoting their status and later each individual in the unit was given a badge or medal to be worn on the right side of the chest for formal occasions. The award was highly desired and coveted by Soviet Red Army units or regiment members. The Germans recognized the Guard's banners as an elite force and targeted them in order to receive their own rewards from Hitler. Some historians view the designation as a form of propaganda by Stalin's Soviet government to deter military mutiny and encourage higher performances. America's version now of a Guards unit would be the Army Rangers or the Navy Seals.

Authors note: There is conflicting information regarding the status of Guards award for the 586th regiment as well as other awards most commonly received for lesser accomplishments. Some sources say the 586th had been nominated to receive the honors, had prepared the documents, commissions recommendations, and photos; however, all supporting paperwork mysteriously disappeared. Rumors circulated that former Commander of the 586th, Kazarinova, had access to the files and destroyed them, perhaps in retaliation for her earlier dismissal from the regiment. One might also suspect her in the same kind of retaliation toward the regimental pilots who should have received the Hero of the Soviet Union award.

The 587th Bomber Aviation Regiment

The 587th was the last regiment to leave Engels and was commanded by Marina Raskova. This was a larger regiment than the other two and also utilized both men and women. Initially the crews selected for this unit trained on the old, outdated Sukhoi SU-2 planes, a single engine light bomber. Raskova used her influence and connections to get twenty brand new twin-engine Petlyakov Pe-2 bombers. The regiment had to wait for the delivery of the aircraft then had to train the pilots and navigators to fly them, as well as the mechanics and crew to service them.

Petlyakov Pe-2 bombers.

These were far superior aircraft compared to the old SU-2 planes. The Pe-2 bomber had four machine guns and was capable of carrying 3,520 pounds of bombs. Top speed was 360 m.p.h. One small problem, the planes were not built with women pilots in mind. The cockpits were larger with the distance to the rudder pedals longer than most women's short legs; blocks were glued to the pedals so the women could reach them and pillows were tucked behind them to shorten the distance. Pilots of the Pe-2 had to operate the throttle with the left hand and pull the stick back with the right hand. With the plane fully loaded with bombs, the stick took extra muscle to pull back at takeoff. The navigator often assisted the pilot in pulling the stick back on takeoffs or pushed her feet against the pilot's seat to give her a brace to pull against. One or two pillows might also have been used under a pilot's bottom to lift her up so she could see over the cockpit and through the windscreen.

These planes required a crew of three: pilot, navigator/

Pe-2 crew preparing for a mission.

bombardier and rear gunner/radio operator. Because extra crew was required for these aircraft, Raskova included men into this regiment, usually in the position of machine gunners, until more women could be trained and assigned. The gunner position required a tall person to operate the rear machine gun; most of the young women recruits were not tall enough so men were assigned as combination gunner and radio operator. A few squabbles initially occurred between the men and women, but under Raskova's command, they quickly dissipated.

Once trained on the Pe-2 bombers, the 587th was assigned to daylight missions of offensive bombing which included attacking enemy positions, destroying their installations and strongholds, harassing troop concentrations, bombing enemy ammunition dumps, transport lines, and artillery batteries.

It was now late December 1942. The pressure was on Raskova to get her new aircraft loaded with bombs and in the air to strike and hold the Germans back from their advances on Stalingrad. Weather was a major factor in flight delays at this time of year. The planes and their crew were ready, but the weather grounded them with snowstorm after relentless storm. A few planes managed to takeoff headed for Stalingrad when visibility was marginal, but they were often forced to land before they could get to their destination due to weather related visibility or engine problems along the way.

On January 4, 1943 Marina and her crew finally took advantage of a break in the weather and departed with two other Pe-2s flying in formation headed for an airfield near Stalingrad. After flying for several hours, the formation became engulfed in thick clouds and heavy fog which reduced visibility to near zero and caused disorientation. Due to the frigid temperatures, icing on the wings may have also been a problem (icing would cause the aircraft to quickly lose altitude and likely crash).

Darkness was fast approaching. The three aircraft had to attempt forced landings somewhere near the banks of the Volga River, with the ground barely visible below them. Two of the planes and their crew crash-landed safely with only minor injuries, but Raskova's plane flew into the top of a cliff ejecting and killing her and her crew instantly.

Due to the severe weather, it took two days for searchers to reach the crash site and recover the bodies. Since she was flying a military mission, her death was considered as KIA (killed in action).

News of Marina Raskova's tragic death quickly spread across the Soviet Union leaving a dark storm of sadness and despair. The sadness arose upon learning of the death of a national heroine. There was also deep sadness and fear for the possible loss of the hopes and dreams Marina had for women in aviation. Feelings of despair and hopelessness the Soviets felt increased as the relentless Germans continued to ravage their beloved Motherland.

Marina, at the age of thirty, received the first State funeral of the Great Patriotic War. Thousands attended as well as many high ranking government officials. Her ashes were inurned in the Kremlin Wall beside her fellow Rodina pilot, Polina Osipenko. Marina was survived by her twelve-year-old daughter and her mother.

Raskova's untimely death and subsequent funeral was reported in America via *The New York Times* as an "impressive ceremony." The newspaper's description detailed the funeral oration delivered by Lieutenant General Aleksandr Scherbakov, head of the Political Department of the Red Army: *"...crowds filed past the urn in which remains rested in the domed hall of the Civil Aviation Club. Before massively banked commemorative wreaths a Guard of Honor stood. Major Raskova's mother was present, but her twelve-year-old daughter was not...General Scherbakov's oration was broadcast throughout Russia, as were Chopin's Funeral March and the Internationale. Banners were dipped and officers stood at salute as an airplane flew low over Red Square."*

Raskova was posthumously awarded the Order of Patriotic War 1st Class. Her regiment was given Guards distinction and was renamed "The 125th M.M. Raskova Borisov Guards Dive Bomber Aviation Regiment," in her honor. Several streets and schools were also renamed in her honor and remain so to this day.

Pravda newspaper from Moscow, June 10, 1943 ran the following short article: *"The American Committee for Aid to the Soviet Union in the war against Nazi Germany announced that on June 22, 1943 a supply ship would be launched at one of the wharves in California. It would be named "Marina Raskova" in memory of the heroic Russian Air Force pilot."*

Author's note: Similar yet somewhat conflicting information was also found regarding the naming of an American ship in the Pravda *article. An article written by Diane Sheean appeared in the* Soviet Russia Today *magazine in June 1943, during "Tribute to Russia Week" in the U.S. The magazine was published in the U.S. by the Friends of the Soviet Union and supported by the lobbying group Russian War Relief. The article described a new Liberty ship which was launched from Los Angeles christened* Marina Raskova. *This historic event made it "the first American ship to be named for a Russian."*

Other information rebuts the Pravda *article altogether by indicating the Ironclad-type American ship was actually launched in April 1919 as the Mystic and transported supplies to the Soviets, our allies at the time. The Americans transferred ownership of the ship to the Soviets in June 1943 where it was renamed the SS Marina Raskova.*

In any case, the point should be made that Marina Raskova was recognized and honored world-wide at that time for her achievements in women's aviation.

Members of the three regiments formed by Raskova openly wept and mourned the loss of their leader, fearing without her leadership the regiments would be disbanded. They were not. Each continued to serve for the duration of the war. Each of the young women vowed to carry on the goals Marina had established for them elevating her to iconic status in their eyes. They referred to themselves as members of Raskova's Regiments. One of the regiment pilots, Golina Brok-Beltsova, was later quoted as she remembered the impact Marina had on her fellow pilots, "For inspiration we had a portrait of Raskova at our base, and we each carried a picture of her in a pocket on the leg of our flight suits. The pocket has a clear covering over it, so we could see her picture. We all called ourselves, *Raskovsi*, belonging to Raskova. She was brave, and so we were brave."

Major Valentin Markov was ordered to take command of the 587th bomber regiment after Marina's death. He was recovering from battle wounds suffered earlier and was not happy about being assigned to a regiment that included women. He made it clear to the women upon his arrival, "There will be no sort of allowances made because you are women, so don't expect them." He came aboard as rough and tough, but in the end he was well respected as their leader, often referred to as *batya,* dad.

Years after the war reflecting on his command, Major Markov stated, "During the war there was no difference between this regiment and any male regiments. We lived in dugouts, as did the other regiments and flew on the same missions, no more or less dangerous."

Marina Raskova's life was short but forever etched in Soviet and world history for her efforts in women's aviation. First recognized as a Soviet heroine, following her death she was elevated to martyr status by her nation's citizens. Her early distance and altitude records have long since been overtaken by others, but she held them first. Her Rodina flight is still recognized and celebrated across her vast nation. Her successful formation of the three female fighter aviation regiments during the war inspired American and British women to create similar units (WASPs - Women Airforce Service Pilots - in America and ATA - Air Transport Auxiliary - British). The WASP and ATA members were not authorized by their governments to fly combat missions. The women were only allowed to ferry planes for the military within their respective countries.

Without her actions and accomplishments, there would not have been much interest in women's aviation in the Soviet Union, nor would there have been women combat air regiments during WWII. Marina was an inspiration to thousands and thousands of young girls and women who have since pursued dreams and careers in aviation.

Postage stamp honoring Marina Raskova after her death.

Despite Marina's tragic and untimely death, her 587th regiment went on to fly 1,134 combat missions for the duration of the Great Patriotic War, dropped over 980,000 tons of bombs, were recognized by the Soviet Union for extraordinary service and received the coveted Guards designation in 1943. Five of its pilots were awarded Hero of the Soviet Union. Sadly, forty-seven flight crew members died at the hands of the enemy.

Chapter 9

The 588th Night Bomber Regiment

The third and most notable regiment formed under the direction of Marina Raskova was the 588th Night Bomber Aviation Regiment, unofficially known as "Stalin's Falcons." As a tribute to Raskova after her death and in recognition for outstanding service to their country, the 588th was awarded the elite status of "Guards" on February 8, 1943 and re-designated the 46th Guards Night Bomber Aviation Regiment, the first all female unit to receive the Guards status. The 588th also had the most highly decorated members of the three regiments. This regiment became the distinguished and memorable *"Nachthexen,"* Night Witches. The term was coined by the Germans as a result of the regiment's successful and deadly attacks upon them at night.

The 588th regiment was tasked with assaulting bridges the enemy was using to move deeper into Soviet territories, bombing enemy strongholds, troop concentrations, fuel and ammunition supplies, vehicles, tanks, and small buildings. They were highly credited with the constant nighttime harassment attacks of German troops which denied them rest and recovery from daytime battles.

This group of pilots, navigators, gunners, mechanics, armorers, and support crew was the only one of the three regiments to remain all female throughout the war.

Raskova appointed Lieutenant Colonel Yevdokiia Bershanskaya *(alternate sources list spelling as Evdokiia Bershanskaia)* Commander of the 588th. She had been an airline pilot for ten years, then an instructor at an aviation school prior to receiving her invitational request to join Raskova's  group. Although she was reluctant to accept the position, she was honored to have been personally asked by Raskova. Bershanskaya was unaccustomed to giving orders and unfamiliar with strict military discipline but had ideas of her own for commanding a group of young women pilots.

The Commander began an innovative training program that would supply continual replacements for her flying personnel when needed. Her idea was thought to be unorthodox at the time; however, it enabled the unit never to be taken out of action on the front lines due to illness or accidents. The training program was simple - train recruits from the bottom then move them up. New volunteers without pilot experience would be trained as support crew then armorers, armorers would then be trained as mechanics, mechanics would be trained as navigators, navigators as pilots. Those who chose to remain in mechanic or armorer positions were allowed to do so. The majority of volunteer recruits were already pilots, many with high-flight hours. Pilots with lower flight hours would be placed in navigator positions, then moved up to pilot positions when needed or when more aircraft were made available. Once the program began, it resulted in a continuously successful operational unit for over three years. No other regiment, including male units, could claim the same success, nor did any utilize this training technique.

Staff members of the 588th.
Note: Chief of Staff Irina Rakobolskaya
center bottom row.

Another innovative idea encouraged by Chief of Staff Irina Rakobolskaia *(alternate sources list spelling as Rakobolskaya)* and authorized by Bershanskaya, was to service and rearm the planes as a crew group instead of individually. Military regulations stated that each single mechanic and armorer was to service their own assigned plane. The new idea was for crew members to direct incoming planes to their hardstands where mechanics would quickly refuel them while teams of armorers would lift bombs into place. There would be several teams of three armorers as well as several teams of two or three mechanics and support crew.

Utilizing this technique, a group of three armorers would work together to arm a returning aircraft. One armorer would unwind the lead from the delivered supply, pass it to the next two who held it at each end then quickly and carefully walked it to the aircraft. Next, they would attach the fuse which armed the bomb then lift the seventy to one hundred pound device up and into the bomb rack under the lower wing. This activity was quickly repeated three more times for a total of four bombs racked into place on each plane. On a busy night, a single armorer would have carried and lifted nearly three tons of bombs by herself, now the load was thankfully shared. Having the three armorers working together reduced injury and fatigue as well as saved time. The team of three armorers would then move to the next incoming aircraft and repeat their actions. Likewise, the team of mechanics checked and fueled the aircraft while crew directed and monitored the traffic of incoming and outgoing aircraft.

This new system enabled an aircraft to be refueled and rearmed within five minutes (think Nascar pit stop!). Don't forget, this was all done in the dark of night with minimal, if any, light.

Bershanskaya was well-respected and genuinely liked by her regiment and later singled out by military higher-ups as one of twelve "remarkable Air Regiment Commanders." She reminded her troops of Raskova with her stern determined and attractive looks, her strong character, non-stop energy, her wonderful smile and words of encouragement. She was self-controlled and modest.

Of the three organized regiments, the 588th, had the poorest equipment or no equipment. Their assigned aircraft were leftover WWI Polikarpov Po-2 open-cockpit biplanes.

The Po-2 open-cockpit biplane.

The biplanes were used in WWI primarily for aerial reconnaissance. After the war, many had been used by the flying clubs for flight training or crop dusting on collective farms. From their crop dusting days, the little planes were often referred to as *kukuruzhnik,* corn cutters, for their ability to fly very low and very slow. They were not in the best of shape, but there were thousands of them available. Many of the recruits were familiar with the Po-2s since those were the planes they learned to fly at their flying clubs after mastering gliders.

The little planes measured twenty-seven feet long and thirty-seven feet wingtip to wingtip, weighing in at 1,700 pounds, empty. They were powered by a Shvetsov M-11 one-hundred horsepower, five cylinder radial engine that sounded like an overworked sewing machine - tata-tata-tata-tata. When the engine was turned off during the night-time dive bombing missions, a soft rustling or swooshing sound could be heard as the slipstream rushed over the wings, through the struts and bracing wires. The planes could glide farther than any other combat planes of that time.

The small engine was only capable of lifting off the ground with a maximum load weight of 3,000 pounds which left a mere 1,300 pounds for the two crew (pilot and navigator), fuel, and ordinance.

These aircraft were slower than most modern cars. Maximum speed for the Po-2 was 82 knots or about 94 m.p.h. while cruising speed was 59 knots, about 68 m.p.h. Because the planes were so slow and maneuverable they could takeoff or land on a three-hundred yard runway. Rarely was a paved runway available, however, cow pastures, clearings, meadows, and dirt roads were most commonly utilized. The wheels could be fitted with skis when the ground was covered in snow and ice, floats for anticipated water landings, or double-wide wheel rims for muddy areas.

Made of wood and canvas, the planes were very light, lacked advanced instruments—a fuel gauge, air speed indicator, compass, and altimeter were standard instruments, none of which were illuminated—no radio, and no parachutes for the pilot or navigator.

Few parachutes were available at the beginning of the war. Because they added extra weight to the planes, the

588th regiment pilots were initially told they did not need them. They were also told they would not be flying at high enough altitudes to warrant parachutes - it was more important to carry bombs.

An acrylic-type windscreen or windshield protected the pilot and navigator from prop wash, wind and debris hitting them in the face. There was no protective cover or canopy on these open cockpit planes.

Without a radio there was no communication with fellow pilots or home base. Most of the planes had an interphone or intercom for pilot to navigator communications. This primitive device consisted of a long, hollow rubber tube with a cup-like apparatus at each end in which one would either shout into or listen from. Remember playing with two soup cans and a string - similar technology of yesteryear!

The plane's wood frame was very old and dry. The canvas wings were heavily coated with "dope"—a thick lacquer used to stiffen and tighten the wing fabric. Most of the planes used by the airborne regiments had been painted in a grey-green camouflage scheme which made them difficult to spot when flying treetop level. Because of the dry wood, multiple coats of dope, and the paint, the planes were highly flammable when hit by any type of enemy fire. The little planes were often referred to as flying matchboxes, flying coffins, or tinder boxes.

The planes were definitely not fighter planes, nor were they designed to be bombers. Initially, after mechanics carefully checked each plane for airworthiness, four small bomb racks were installed under the lower wings, two on each side of the fuselage. A strong wire cable was attached to each rack and threaded up into the two cockpits. The pilot or navigator would pull on the cable to open the racks and drop the bombs. The planes carried up to four bombs weighing seventy to two hundred-twenty pounds each, not to exceed a total weight of seven hundred-seventy pounds. These were considered small bombs in comparison to larger aircraft capable of carrying larger and much heavier ordinance. Utilizing the smaller bombs was ideal for the type of attack missions assigned to the regiment as mentioned earlier.

Later in the war, lightweight machine guns were mounted and bolted to the aircraft frame behind the rear cockpit. Navigators were not thrilled with this addition to their workload. Their seat faced forward and the gun pointed backward. In order to operate the gun, the navigator had to unbuckle her restraint harness, turn around on her knees, take aim and shoot. A bit precarious to say the least.

Before the women assigned to the 588th could take to the air for frontline combat missions, they received three additional months of training at Engels in nighttime combat, dive bombing, and formation flying techniques. Navigators were also instructed in how to maintain orientation during very low altitude flying, which the regiment and their slow aircraft were assigned to carry out. Unfortunately, during this training time, two planes with their pilot and navigator in each were killed.

In late May 1942, the 588th finally received their orders to move forward and into position on the front. The Garrison Commander at Engels, Colonel Bagaev, had never been much in favor of the entire Raskova concept of an all women regiment and often referred to the women as his "little princesses." He called the women together for a short speech prior to their departure:

"Today, for the first time, a women's regiment leaves our airfield for the front. You do not fly on awesome machines, but on training aircraft. And it's true that you yourselves are not excessively awesome in appearance. But I am certain that in these light-winged airplanes, you will be able to inflict heavy blows on the enemy. Let fly with you my fatherly wish: success to you and combat glory!"

From then on, the 588th Regiment was constantly on the move, ordered to bomb moving German strongholds primarily on the Southern Front as well as the Western Front - Prussia, Belorussia, Poland, the Crimea, and Berlin. Wherever the front line need was the greatest, the women were there, fully operational until the end of the Great Patriotic War. This unit was the most cohesive of Marina Raskova's three regiments most likely due to the effective and innovative leadership of Bershanskaya and Rakobolskaia.

The 588th Night Bomber Regiment

From May 1942 to May 1945, during 1,100 nights of combat, the 46th Taman Guards Night Bomber Aviation Regiment (the 588th) flew over 24,000 combat missions, dropped more than 23,000 tons of bombs with twenty-three regiment pilots and navigators receiving the coveted Hero of the Soviet Union honor. The 46th Guards pilots and their navigators each had an average of over 700 flights with one pilot, Irina Sebrova, logging 1,008 combat flights. Very few male regiments could boast these accomplishments, or even came close.

Author's note: The Hero of the Soviet Union (HSU) award has been mentioned several times thus far. The HSU award during the Great Patriotic War, the highest award for valor, was only conferred upon a pilot or navigator who had completed more than five hundred successful combat missions. Infantry, partisans, spies, and resistance workers were also honored for their deeds and service to the Soviet Union and society. The medal itself (seen below) was a gold star held by a red ribbon. The star was engraved on the back with the sequential number of presentation. The HSU recipients may be awarded a second medal for additional feats of heroism or valor in which case a bronze bust of his or her likeness would also be cast with an inscription commemorating the feat(s) and erected in his or her hometown.

During the Great Patriotic War, a total of 11,633 HSU medals were awarded. Of those, 2,332 were for aviation feats, primarily earned by the women of Raskova's regiments of which sixty-one of them received double awards. Interestingly enough, my research found few, if any, complete lists of the women receiving these awards. Only after reading the history of each individual could I find the number of awards they received. Perhaps an example of the award being given to the women but not publicized?

The award was abolished in 1991 with the change in the political climate of the Soviet Union.

The British equivalent is the Victoria Cross. The American equivalent is the Medal of Honor.

Chapter 10

"Tonight We Fly!"

When the departure date from Engels for the 588th arrived in late May 1942, it was greeted with anxiety and anticipation of what was to come for the young women. The full regiment of pilots, navigators, mechanics, armorers, and support crew were packed up and ready to go to their first assignment. All were gathered at attention on the flight line and heard Colonel Bagaev's speech. Then Marina Raskova slowly walked the line smiling at each, with a few words of encouragement here and there. She was like a proud mom sending her children off to their first day of school. After she passed the entire assembled group, she turned and gave a short speech. Marina flashed her beautiful smile and told them how proud she was of each and every one of them, how they had all come a long way in such a short time, and how they were now aviation soldiers. She saluted and dismissed them shouting, "Happy skies, happy skies!" It would be the last time she saw any of them again and the last time they, in turn, would ever see her again.

Pilots and navigators rushed to their planes and climbed aboard pulling on their leather helmets and goggles. They had already completed their preflight checks and had their maps in the cockpits ready to go. The mechanics and support crew climbed aboard their assigned transport aircraft which also carried the regiment's gear and belongings. The noise was deafening as nearly fifty aircraft roared to life and began taxiing into position for takeoff. The Po-2s would liftoff first followed by the transport aircraft. Once in the air, the Po-2s gathered in two groups of a loose "V" formation then climbed to an altitude of 5,000 feet. Commander Yevdokiia Bershanskaya flew the lead aircraft, while the transport aircraft followed behind the two formations. All were headed south from Engels to an assigned area near Stalingrad.

After peacefully flying and enjoying the views of the countryside for nearly an hour, three fighter aircraft suddenly screamed by the two formations in an apparent attack mode. Several of the 588th pilots immediately took evasive action and placed their aircraft in steep dives headed for a low altitude cover. The majority of the Po-2s continued to hold their positions and flew on. Without radios in their aircraft those taking evasive action had no clue what was going on. Why were they being attacked? Why didn't the attackers fire at them? Didn't the others see the attack planes? When they felt it was safe to do so they regained altitude, caught up with the two formations, continued on to their destination, and landed safely.

Upon arrival at their assigned base, the pilots immediately reported to Bershanskaya what had happened. She was fit to be tied! The "attacking aircraft" were their own Soviet fighters sent to escort them to their new airfield! The women were ashamed and embarrassed for not recognizing their own counterparts. The men flying the fighters were quickly reprimanded by their commander for unsafe flight tactics. They had been overheard laughing and boasting about how they had scared the "girlie" pilots by diving into their formation in hopes the girls would be sent elsewhere. This was not the way for the 588th to start their first assignment.

Once all of the regiment had arrived, transport trucks appeared to take them to their quarters. Unfortunately, the tiny airfield had no five star hotels on or near the premises. The women were to be separated from the men, which suited all concerned just fine. The transport trucks lumbered along a bumpy, rutted cow path near the airfield and pulled up to a large empty barn. Imagine the dismay as the women entered the malodorous, filthy barn and realized this was their new home. Undaunted, they pushed up their sleeves and immediately set to work sweeping, scrubbing, cleaning, and disinfecting to make the place habitable. Despite their best efforts, the odor was not completely eliminated but was slightly less disgusting. At least they had a roof over their heads, although probably leaky, and they were thankful for a place to sleep. They named their first new abode, "The Inn of the Flying Cow!"

For two weeks the regiment flew night and day training missions and reconnaissance to familiarize themselves with the area and its terrain. They studied available maps and began planning their strategy for bombing runs. They also studied and reviewed aircraft recognition—the difference between German and Soviet fighters and bombers!

Raskova had trained them well at Engels to fly low and slow but to always stay alert for tall obstacles, trees, and buildings. Night flying was extremely dangerous, but they made adjustments and learned to read light and

Squadron pilots reviewing maps.

dark shadows. Flying when a full moon was brightest often played visual tricks on them; tall trees took on frightful forms, low lines of shrubs looked like enemy soldiers lying in wait. The pilot had to be able to maneuver the aircraft in a split second while the navigator was to keep track of where they were headed, watch for enemy fighters surprising them from behind, and how to return to home base.

The attack strategy was to approach targets from downwind, if possible, so the aircraft noise would be carried away from the target. Target approach would be from an altitude of 3,000 feet at which time the engine would be cut and the aircraft placed in a steep, fast gliding dive. The navigator would toss out two flares suspended by mini-parachutes. The magnesium flares would ignite and burst into a bright, white light illuminating the target area. Bombs would be dropped beginning at an altitude of 1,300 feet, engine quickly re-started, aircraft pulled up and away sharply, then returned to base.

Pilots had to be aware of the aircraft's reaction when the bombs were released as well as when the bombs struck their target. Upon release, the plane would shutter or wobble a bit from loss of the bomb weight. Once the bombs hit the target, an invisible shock wave would push the small plane upward. If the pilot did not anticipate these reactions, she could lose control of the aircraft very quickly, become disoriented and lose her flight direction. Bombing at less than 1,300 feet had the potential of shrapnel and debris from the blast hitting the airplane and setting it on fire.

Weather was also a factor in maintaining control of the aircraft. Strong winds could easily blow the small, lightweight aircraft off course. Updrafts and downdrafts could also prove deadly when flying near hilly terrain or mountain ranges. Rain and snow was miserable in an open cockpit plane, oftentimes affecting visibility which could cause disorientation.

Planes would fly in groups or waves of three, three to five minutes apart. The lead aircraft threw out the flares while the following two utilized the light from the exploding bombs as their targets. The Germans would quickly turn on their searchlights and begin firing at the first aircraft just as the second and third aircraft would drop their bomb loads to, hopefully, knock out the search light and artillery. The second wave of bombers would dive in and continue the attack utilizing the fires burning from the first wave's attack as a target.

Since the little Po-2s were short range aircraft, the regiments were stationed as close to the front lines, or advancing enemy lines, as possible (sometimes less than a mere twenty-five miles away) which enabled the regiment's squadrons to fly repeated night-time missions but also subjected them to discovery by the Germans. That discovery led to frequent, unexpected changes in airfield bases. "Airfields" was a misnomer as mentioned earlier. Airfields were most often a large open field or pasture, not a well-stocked or fueled airport with a paved runway, hangars and pilot quarters. Base-of-operations would probably be a better term.

Late in the afternoon of June 8, 1942, the two 588th squadrons were called together for a briefing. Bershanskaya passed out updated maps with targets and routes marked and discussed the plan of attack. Ground crews were told to fuel and ready twenty aircraft. This seemed like a normal briefing

A squadron briefing prior to a flight mission.

the squadrons had been receiving every day for practice until the tone of Bershanskaya's voice suddenly changed. With loud, stern words she added, "Arm the planes! Tonight we fly!"

There were a few seconds of silence as if they had to process what was just said, then whoops and cheers spread quickly through the group. Nervous laughter and chattering could be heard as all the young women scattered to prepare for their first actual combat mission. Beneath that nervous laughter and chatter was subdued and suppressed, cold, hard fear.

The first three planes to takeoff would have Commander Yevdokiia Bershanskaya and her navigator in the lead. The second plane would have Luba Olkovskaya and her navigator, with Anya Amosova and her navigator in the third plane. Bershanskaya assigned this group to be the first out as they were her most experienced pilot/navigator crews. She also felt, as their Commander, she should be the one to lead them on their first actual mission.

When darkness blanketed the area, the little Po-2s were loaded, armed and ready for their mission. Pilots, navigators and crew had sweaty hands and pounding hearts as each waited for their launch call. The target was the headquarters of a German tank division behind the front line near Voroshilovgrad. The Germans would not be used to an attack at night behind their advancing lines where their reserve soldiers rested, supplies were stored, and the regiment headquarters might be staged. This became the signature strategy for attack by the 588th: night-time surprise attacks of revenge for their Motherland and as a tribute to their beloved Marina Raskova.

The attack went well taking the Germans completely by surprise and causing significant damage. It took the Germans a bit of time to turn their searchlights on and frantically fire their anti-aircraft guns. The first and third planes returned safely to base but the second plane did not.

Olkovskaya's plane was hit by flak from the anti-aircraft guns, caught fire and crashed killing her and her navigator. Once again, the young women were devastated by the news of losing two more from their regiment. Bershanskaya quickly rallied them into position for the second mission of the night. Twenty additional planes bombed a Soviet railway the Germans had overtaken and were utilizing for supplies, as well as an artillery battery moving closer to Stalingrad. All twenty returned to base safely, many with bullet and flak holes in their aircraft. Several of the pilots had their crew paint the sides of their aircraft with the following:

Mest' vragu za smert' nashikh druzey
Revenge to the Enemy for the Death of our Friends

The first missions flown by the 588th created a great deal of German outrage - visualize the proverbial "rock into a hornet's nest!" They had prepared and adapted to being attacked during the day, on the ground or in the air, but definitely not deep into the night, nor struck in their flank positions. The women took advantage of this and continued to hit them hard every night, all night, from early June to late July. Consequently, the German advance on Stalingrad was not going well; they were attacked relentlessly day and night with the night-time missions causing them the most harm. The night-time attacks, known as "harassment bombing," inflicted psychological terror among the Germans. When they learned the bombers were women, the Germans were even more demoralized and outraged.

Catching on to the routine of the night bombers, the German officers issued orders to their troops banning all types of light sources after dark: no cigarettes, no candles, no flashlights, no cooking over a flame or stove, no fires for warmth. It was thought that eliminating light sources would decrease night-time targets. It did not. When an attack was expected or imminent, the German radios would frantically announce, *"Achtung! Achtung!..."* "Attention! Attention, the ladies are in the air, stay at your shelters." After the war, one German Luftwaffe flying ace, Hauptmann Johannes Steinhoff, wrote, "We simply could not grasp that the Soviet airmen that caused us the greatest trouble were in fact WOMEN. These women feared nothing. They came night after night in their very slow biplanes, and for some periods they wouldn't give us any sleep at all."

To feel more prepared for night-time attacks from the "lady bombers" the Germans arranged their artillery guns and searchlights during the day in a camouflaged circle around probable targets. The Soviets called this German maneuver a "flak circus." When the first planes crossed the perimeter of the circus, the searchlights would be snapped

Searchlights

on to blind them while the anti-aircraft guns fired at them. It was a great idea, however, the 588th continued to fly in their formations of three with the aforementioned attack plan: approach targets from downwind so any aircraft sounds would be carried away from the target, lead planes were decoys to distract the searchlights then turned quickly and sharply to avoid being hit while the others snuck in and dropped their bomb loads. Hopefully, the searchlights were taken out on the first run. With a quick turnaround to re-arm and the searchlights destroyed, the women continued their surprise attacks through the night. As a result, the Germans suffered heavy losses of men, supplies and equipment.

The German anti-aircraft guns caused the most fear for the night bombers. Although the artillery was usually located near search lights, the Germans might station a battery elsewhere within their encampment to fire at the unsuspecting aircraft. The guns utilized 88 mm shells, in most cases,

German anti-aircraft guns

that would explode at different altitudes. Every five rounds had a tracer shell which was packed with a pyrotechnic charge. The charge would ignite and a tail of white or red light could be seen shooting into the sky. At night the tracers aided the shooters in adjusting their aim at the aircraft passing overhead. Tracers also caused momentary blindness to the pilots as the bright lights flashed past their aircraft.

For the Po-2 pilots and their navigators, being shot at by anti-aircraft guns was like flying through a lightening storm. The shells exploded around them and sent flak, burning metal fragments from the exploded shells, in all directions at very high speed. When they exploded, little puffs of brown or white smoke filled the air. Smoke from the exploded shells, as well as smoke from the exploded bombs, quickly surrounded and choked the two women in their open cockpits. The smoke smelled like a combination of sulfur from fireworks and the sharp, chemical smell of dynamite; it clung to their clothing and was not easily washed out. The heavy smoke burned and irritated their eyes, which reduced visibility as they tried to maintain their flight course and return to base.

In late 1942, the Germans began using a better ground based radar system to locate approaching enemy aircraft. When an aircraft was detected on radar, the searchlights were turned and pointed in their oncoming direction with anti-aircraft guns firing along the same line. This tactic was somewhat unsuccessful in deterring the 588th pilots. The non-reflective canvas and wood surfaces of their planes were not picked up by radar. The planes also flew so low and slow they were not detected by the ground radar. Because of the minimal heat emissions from the Po-2s small 110-hp engines, German fighter planes equipped with infrared heat seekers also had difficulties locating them.

Shortly after the 588th began their night-time attacks, they acquired their nicknames from the Germans. German soldiers had discovered from the villagers and partisans that the night bombers were actually Soviet women pilots. This infuriated them! As mentioned earlier, the soft rustling or swooshing sound the planes made as they dove to their targets, without their sewing machine sounding motors running, created the auditory vision of a fairytale witch flying through the night sky on her broom. Hence, the Germans referred to them as *Nachthexen,* Night Witches. The nickname soon attached itself to any Soviet airwoman, not just the pilots of the 588th. The Germans also named the 588th's planes *Nahmaschine,* sewing machines. When news of the Night Witches "title" reached the young women they were highly offended at first, "We are not witches! We are doing our job." The anger slowly dissipated and turned into pride as the women realized the Germans feared them and their nightly raids. In fact, some German soldiers thought these pilots really were sorceresses or witches and were afraid to shoot at them, or shoot them down from the sky, for fear that a black magic spell might be cast upon them. However, the Witches own Soviet infantry gratefully called them *Nebesnyye Sushchestva,* Heavenly Beings.

Chapter 11

Life in the Coven

When the Red Air Force needed more support from the 588th in a different location, the regiment quickly pulled up stakes and literally dug in at a new home base. Upon arrival, if no structures were available for accommodations, the women dug deep trenches and covered them with old boards or logs, soil and sod, large rocks, or whatever was available. The freshly dug dirt had a pleasant earthy smell at first, but soon the dugout became stuffy and smokey, then rancid from body odor. An old oil drum was placed in the center of their trench dugout as a heat stove to keep them warm in cold weather. Smoke was vented out with a wide pipe through the "roof."

The dugout dirt "floor" would be covered with several inches of water when it rained and quickly became a muddy, uncomfortable mess. Beds were planks of wood with the women's blankets and pillows atop them. Wet bedding and clothing was difficult to dry and usually took several days. Wet boots placed near an open fire or heat stove to dry were often later found melted or burnt and unwearable.

There were no elaborately decorated bathrooms with plush hand towels or fancy, soft toilet paper. Instead, a deep hole was dug away from base activity near large bushes or trees. A plank with a large circle cut into it was placed over the hole. On rare occasions the hole was covered with a "privacy hut" similar to an outhouse. When a base was shared with male regiments, separate "facilities" were made available with a privacy hut for each.

Running water sources were rare at most of the airbase sites. River water or melted snow had to suffice for drinking, cooking, washing clothing, and bathing. Empty metallic detonator boxes were used to heat water for a quick wash of hands and face. After a bombing mission, the smell of smoke clung to flight suits, exposed hair and skin. A nice soak in a hot bathtub after a mission was always a dream. Bathing was a luxury. A frigid dunk in a nearby river or stream was considered a bath. If a nearby friendly village had a bathhouse, a transport truck would collect the women from their base and drive them to the village. Soap or shampoo was a scarce luxury, but a deep soak in a tub filled with hot water worked wonders—the wartime version of a spa day for the girls!

Winters were brutal for everyone. Snow and ice storms often prevented any flight activity. The planes had no cover or warm insulated hangars to protect them from the storms. Special precautions had to be adhered to in sub-zero weather to protect both planes and crew. Heavy wool blankets were often used to cover the engines and cockpits but were easily blown off by the wind. The crews started the planes at intervals and let the engines idle for several minutes to prevent them from freezing. Although this was a waste of fuel it was a necessity to prevent the loss of an aircraft engine.

Mechanics and armorers suffered the most when preparing the planes for a mission. Bundled in their heavy winter clothing it was difficult enough to walk let alone fuel and arm the planes.

Flying in sub-zero weather was also hazardous to the pilots and navigators. There were no onboard heaters in the cockpits. The little Po-2 open cockpit aircraft only had windscreens in front of the pilot and navigator. Ducking ones head out from behind the windscreen into the frigid slipstream risked frostbite to the face, especially the nose. When the navigator had to drop flares over a bomb site, she had to lean out over the edge of the plane. The freezing slipstream felt like a thousand needles slamming into her face and took her breath away. Multiple missions in these conditions also caused frostbite to the toes and feet.

When the planes returned to base between the freezing cold missions, crew provided hot tea to pilots and their navigators in an effort to help warm them. They rushed the hot drink out to the cockpits while the pilot and navigator remained in their aircraft as it was refueled and rearmed for the turnaround mission.

Since the nights were longer during the winter months, more missions could be flown each night when temperatures and weather permitted. It was not uncommon for the regiment to average one hundred flights per night, with each pilot flying twelve to twenty missions. The maximum number of flights in one night for the regiment was recorded at three hundred twenty-five. Depending on the location of the targets, each flight took an average of thirty to fifty minutes with a turnaround time of five minutes or more. Summers had shorter nights and the number of missions per night dropped to an average of eight to ten per pilot.

As sunrise neared and the missions were completed, each pilot and navigator received a four ounce drink of vodka as ordered by the Red Army doctors. This was supposed to help them relax, reduce stress and help them sleep. Those who did not drink alcohol gave their prescribed ration to their mechanics or armorers or traded them vodka for chocolate.

Extreme fatigue and lack of sleep gradually took its toll. The high stress and tension of their dangerous jobs often prevented a deep, restful sleep. Sleep during the daytime was short lived as the noisy activity of the daytime regiment bombers continued. The average number of sleep hours during the day was two to four—the typical night shift workers dilemma, even today.

The extreme fatigue also sent the immune system into a tailspin. Colds, flu, and injuries disrupted their flight schedules. Poor nutrition caused a variety of problems as the war lingered on; weight loss, intestinal upsets, tooth loss, skin lesions, hair difficulties, etc. Inhalation of smoke and gunpowder from the bombing often caused breathing difficulties which lead to asthma-like symptoms, bronchitis or pneumonia. Blinding by searchlights caused visual disturbances which quickly resolved themselves; exploding bombs caused hearing loss, temporary as well as permanent.

The Red Army doctors prescribed stimulants they called Coca-Cola pills (caffeine pills) to combat fatigue. Many of the young women, especially the armorers, did not like to take the pills because they made the women too jittery to do their jobs. The pills also kept them from being able to get to sleep after their work was done.

A few members of the 588th taking a break, singing and dancing.

For rest and relaxation the young women enjoyed knitting, crochet, embroidery, and sewing. Old woolen sweaters were unraveled and repurposed as sorely needed socks and scarves for the sub zero temperatures. Singing cheerful folk songs reminded them of home, while laughing and dancing relieved stress and tension.

It was rare to have a book or magazine available but if one found its way to the regiment, it was readily shared and quickly worn from all the handling. *Pravda* newspapers were a common information source, although filled with propaganda, and were usually weeks or months old. Underground partisan papers usually had more current, reliable information about activities in the local areas and were easier to come by.

Since the regiments moved so often, they were difficult to locate in a timely manner for mail delivery. Letters and packages from loved ones at home took circuitous routes before they finally arrived. Packages often had wool socks, scarves, underwear, soap, bread, or a rare treat of chocolate.

As the war lingered on, food became more and more scarce. The entire regiment often went several days without a substantial meal, just a dry piece of bread or a meatless, watered down soup. Nearby peasants offered milk, potatoes or bread when they could, but they were also starving. Supply planes would land as often as they were able to escape being shot down by the Germans. Fuel, ammunition, bombs, equipment, supplies, and food were quickly off-loaded and stored. Fuel and armament often took priority over food; without fuel the planes could not get off the ground. But without basic nourishment the pilots were not fit to fly - a Catch-22.

Each airbase had some type of guard house where unruly regiment members were confined as punishment for minor infractions or disobedience. The term of punishment was based on the harshness of the crime but usually lasted two to seven days. Crimes usually consisted of not following military orders or protocol, reckless or exhibition flying such as buzzing the field with a low level fast pass or unauthorized aerobatic maneuvers, etc. Often, after a few hours of confinement, the "prisoner" was set free due to need on the flight line or other important duties. Some prisoners viewed the punishment as an opportunity for uninterrupted sleep!

When situations warranted, members of the squadron were called upon to fly day time reconnaissance missions, scouting enemy lines, artillery, tanks, and estimating regiment sizes. They also flew supplies to partisans behind enemy lines as well as transporting sick and wounded to field hospitals or high ranking officials from base to base. The little Po-2s were able to fly low to the ground undetect-

Pilots and navigators reviewing maps for a day time mission.

ed by German radar to accomplish these tasks. Landing and takeoffs in fields or on dirt roads were quick and easy for the little planes, but pilots had to be ever watchful for German snipers on the ground or their fighter planes in the air.

The greatest fear of the young women was not of the anti-aircraft guns, or dying in a crash, instead it was of being captured by the Germans. The fear of being taken prisoner, tortured, or raped by the brutal Germans weighed heavily on their minds as they left on every mission. The women recalled Marina Raskova's instructions when she handed each pilot her own pistol and seven bullets, "Use six to kill the enemy, save one for yourself if needed, aim for your heart."

Neither crashes, injuries, nor illness kept the women from their flight duties. If injured after surviving a crash, they returned to the regiment as soon as they were able and continued where they left off. Also, when illness struck, after a few days rest, they were back to take their turn on the flight line whether they were 100% recovered or not.

These young women were driven by the love of their country and respect for carrying on Marina Raskova's mission. They had lost many of their regimental friends (fifty by the end of the war) as well as their own families and loved ones all due to the Germans and their allies. They had witnessed first hand the ruthless brutality of the Luftwaffe as they strafed and bombed thousands and thousands of fleeing men, women, and children, wiped out villages, burned and looted, tortured, murdered... the list was long. The women thought the best way to revenge these horrors was to continue exacting their own horrors in return, and they did with over 24,000 combat missions flown by the end of the war.

Members
of a
squadron
in the
588th.

Chapter 12

The Witches Revenge

"Revenge to the Enemy for the Death of our Friends" became the Night Witches' flight-fight song. The German Luftwaffe was reputedly the finest fighter group in WWII with the highest ranking fighter aces in history. The Witches were not intimidated by them and continued to fight against them. Each sortie (mission) gave the Witches more confidence in their flight and bombing skills. When news of German attacks on their home villages or deaths of their families or friends reached them, the Witches became even more vengeful, their attacks more ruthless.

From their first combat flight in June through the late months of 1942, the Witches fought the Germans relentlessly to keep them from capturing Stalingrad (the Stalingrad Campaign). In July, the Witches destroyed a railway station and fuel tankers which cut off supplies to the Germans. Extra troops were then sent to bolster the German ranks and deliver fresh supplies. To avoid detection, the German troops crossed the river Don in the dark of night; a grave mistake on their part. The Witches destroyed the German crossing, a motorized unit, and halted further advancement of additional troops. This was successfully accomplished by the Night Witches in forty-six flight missions over two nights of unrelenting bombing.

The Germans were pushed back, away from Stalingrad, during the day by Soviet ground troops, daytime bombers and fighter planes, then constantly harassed all night, every night, by the Witches. Things looked grim for the Germans. Their strong desire to capture Stalingrad seemed to be fading.

On October 25, 1942 the Witches struck the Germans hard at an airfield they controlled near Armavir. One of the Witches' small bombs hit a fuel depot sending a huge fireball hurtling high into the night sky. The little Po-2s were rocked violently from the shock wave caused by the blast, but the Witches held steady and returned for more. The massive fire was like a beacon shouting out to them, "Bomb here!"…and that is exactly what they did. The Witches continued to bomb the airfield and its surroundings as the fire spread. The encampment was in chaos. Seven medium range German bombers were destroyed leaving only one aircraft unscathed. The Germans quickly retreated in defeat to the Kerch Peninsula. This was one of the most destructive missions the Witches had accomplished so far.

In November, the Witches continued to fly missions in support of the Stalingrad Campaign. Many of the missions took them directly over what had once been a beautiful city, now reduced to rubble and picked clean of its valuables by the Germans. For the Witches who had grown up in those areas, it was heartbreaking to see and yet motivating; it gave them a purpose to fight even harder to revenge their Motherland.

The devastating news on January 4, 1943 of Marina Raskova's death, sent a shock wave of sorrow through her three regiments. All were in mourning, devastated at the loss of their beloved leader. But the war did not slow down or stop because of her death. Marina's three regiments continued their duties with a renewed vengeance.

By February 3, 1943 the German's 6th Army had been destroyed. The turning point of the war on the Eastern front came with the surrender of 50,000 German soldiers marching into Soviet captivity, of which 90% would not survive. Many of the prisoners succumbed to the brutality of their captors by starvation, wounds, infections or froze to death in the northern prisons and labor camps. Hundreds of thousands of Germans died from battles in the areas near Stalingrad; their bodies left to decompose where they fell.

Hitler was furious. He wanted to demonstrate his superiority by overtaking Stalingrad and Leningrad only because they were named after Soviet leaders. He also wanted to gain control of the rich oil fields located in the region. That did not happen either.

Hitler's new plan was to withdraw troops from regions where they were being overtaken in an effort to consolidate, and rebuild strength on the Taman Peninsula. As the Germans not captured by Soviet soldiers retreated and headed for the Taman Peninsula, they systematically destroyed bridges, railroads, bombed water wells, and set mines on roadways in an effort to slow the Soviet's pursuit of them.

The Taman Peninsula was located in the Caucasus region of southern Russia. Hitler thought this area would be an ideal position to base operations for rebuilding his troop strength and mounting another offensive aimed at regaining a hold on the rich oil fields.

At the same time, the Soviet army established a strong defensive position in the area to keep the Germans at bay and protect access to the oil fields; they called it the "Blue Line." The Line followed the Kurka River for nearly thirty-five miles and included tributaries, marshes, and thick swampy land. Frequent skirmishes to gain control over the area between the two forces lasted several months. The Germans increased their troop strength and supplies under cover of darkness in an attempt to overtake the Soviets. The Soviet high command finally began plans to completely clear the Taman Peninsula of German occupied forces. They called the plan, the Taman Offensive Operation.

At this point, April 1943, on the Taman Peninsula the Germans only had three hundred aircraft. The Soviets had more than one thousand, which included the 46th Guards Night Bomber Regiment—the Night Witches. One dark and moonless night during a mission to neutralize several anti-aircraft batteries, one of the Night Witches was suddenly caught in the blinding circular beams of ten searchlights; the flak circus or the "Devil's Sabbath," as they called it. The pilot and her navigator knew anti-aircraft fire, tracers, and exploding flak would soon be directed at their aircraft.

The pilot, Katya Piskareva, maintained her course aiming for the largest, brightest searchlight along with its anti-aircraft gun, while her navigator, Raisa Aronova, prepared

Raisa Aronova

to release their bomb load. The Po-2 was suddenly hit by flak, shattering the right lower wing and striking Raisa in the hip just as she was set to release the bombs. Screaming in shock and pain she quickly recovered enough to reach out for the bomb release cables and miraculously managed to see all six bombs hit their intended targets.

At the same time, Katya wrestled with the damaged Po-2 diving close to the ground while trying to get as far from the Germans as she could before attempting a crash landing. Other Night Witch aircrews behind her saw the plane get hit by the anti-aircraft fire, then watched it fall out of sight. They all feared the two had been killed. Each of the crews reported their observations to the commander when they returned to base.

Pilot Piskareva managed to crash-land the plane in friendly territory not far from their base; it took three days for both women to stagger back to the airfield on foot. At first sight of their regiment friends, a loud cheer was heard across the airbase. Although the two were covered in blood from their multiple mission wounds plus cuts and scrapes from their journey back to base, they raised their arms defiantly as if to say, "Mission accomplished!"

For six months on the Taman Peninsula, the Soviets pounded the Germans day and night. On September 10 at 2:00 a.m. the Soviets launched massive artillery barrages, naval torpedo boat strikes, nighttime air strikes from the Witches, followed by daytime air strikes, all aimed at the German encampments. The fighting raged on for a month until October 9 when the last German and Romanian allied soldiers surrendered by pulling out of the Taman Peninsula.

After the Taman battle and surrender, the Germans listed casualties at 10,000 killed, 36,000 wounded, 3,500 missing in action (many of the missing simply fled the area). Romanians listed 1,600 killed, 7,200 wounded, and 800 missing in action. Soviet casualties *(note: various sources list a variety of conflicting numbers)* estimated at 114,000 of which 40,000 were killed.

The Taman Peninsula battle was another blow to the Germans but was a victory for the Soviets thereby ending any future campaigns by Hitler in the Caucasus region. On October 9, 1943 the Night Witches' unit was awarded the honorific "Taman" for facilitating the German defeat on the Taman Peninsula. They were the first all women's air regiment to receive the highly coveted honor. Thereafter, the 588th was known as the 46th Taman Guards Bomber Aviation Regiment.

The Witches Revenge

Author's note: In October 1967, on the Taman Peninsula a monument was unveiled with a dedication ceremony honoring the personnel of the the 46th Taman Guards Bomber Aviation Regiment as well as Soviet Air Force, Red Army soldiers, and sailors that were instrumental in the liberation of the Taman Peninsula.

During the skirmishes leading up to the Taman battle, the Night Witches suffered their most horrific battle loss. On the night of July 31-August 1, 1943, fifteen Po-2s took off on their first mission of the night across the Blue Line. The targets were fairly close to their airfield so the missions would be short thus enabling them to fly quick turn-arounds. Knowing the Witches would soon be attacking, the Germans had searchlights sweeping the sky. As the first plane approached the target area its pilot noticed there was none of the usual anti-aircraft fire. The navigator released her bombs on the targets. The pilot began her turn to avoid the searchlights as she headed back to base. It seemed odd that no artillery fire was tracking them, just the searchlights.

The second plane in formation zeroed in on the target even though they were also caught in the blinding beams of the searchlights. Still no sound of artillery fire from below. Something was definitely odd and out of character for the Germans that particular night.

Suddenly, from high above and bearing down behind the Po-2s at increasing speed came the high pitched scream of a Messerschmitt German fighter plane accompanied by the rata-tat-tat of its machine gun. The bright tracers from the gun were aimed directly at the slow moving Po-2 striking its wing which immediately set the aircraft on fire. The Night Witch pilot tried frantically to sideslip the plane to keep the fire from hitting the engine, but the entire plane burst into flames then slowly spiraled to the ground.

Fear and panic set in and spread quickly to the rest of the Night Witches' formation. The other pilots and their navigators watched in horror as their friends fell to earth burning to death. The Messerschmitt pulled up sharply and went hunting for other victims caught in the strong beams of the searchlights. As the enemy fighter dropped into position behind another Po-2, anti-aircraft fire spewed from below. The Po-2 did not have a chance as the aircraft burst into flames and plummeted to the ground.

Other frenzied Po-2 pilots began to take evasive action by dropping closer to the ground and slowing their airspeed. Since the bombs they carried were armed, they had to be dropped. The pilots and navigators had been instructed never to drop bombs from an altitude of less than 1,000 feet; the Po-2 could not withstand the bomb's explosive shock wave and could be struck by flak from the explosion. The choices in this extreme situation were to maintain altitude, risk being hit by the Messerschmitt and a sudden flaming death or to stay low, drop the bombs and be shaken to death by the shock wave. Most of the Witches chose the later and held on tight. After dropping their bombs they dropped even lower, some at treetop level, to stay clear of the fighter plane and attempt a return to base.

The Messerschmitt could not maneuver as quickly or make the tight turns the small Po-2s were able to nor could it fly at treetop level. Within ten minutes, the fighter plane managed to destroy four of the Po-2s killing all eight of their crew before it disappeared into the night sky.

Fifteen Witches in their Po-2s took off that night, only eleven returned. As the pilots and their navigators returned to base they reported to Major Bershanskaya. She was just as devastated as the others. She ordered the regiment to "stand down" - no further flights that night. The airfield became silent; very little conversation or movement. Everyone was in shock. When the young women slowly made their way to the bunker, another disheartening wave overcame them as they gazed at the eight empty beds and belongings of their deceased friends. The rest of the night was filled with weeping, praying, and fitful sleep.

Several days passed before the women could bring themselves to pack up belongings, enclose notes, and send parcels to the surviving families. There would undoubtedly be more deaths within the regiment but never so many in one night. The regiment was transferred to another area a few days later and continued operations.

The surprise attack by the German Messerschmitt night fighter did not alter the Night Witches basic attack strategies. It did, however, increase their attentiveness to the possibilities of more nighttime attacks and sharpened their low level, evasive flying skills.

Author's note: The Germans had been utilizing night fighters for some time against the British but this was the first attack against the Soviet Night Witches. In addition to the Messerschmitts, Junkers, Dorniers, and the Heinkel aircraft were also flown as night fighters. All of these aircraft were unable to fly completely blind, as the Night Witches did. By mid-1943, these German aircraft were equipped with lights and specialized night flying radar which had recently been perfected. With this radar in working order, the tactic was to find the Soviet enemy bombers and position the fighter behind them, then open fire with their machine guns. Many times the bomber crew never knew they had been attacked until the aircraft heaved, shuttered, or caught fire from the exploding shells. It was basically an airborne sniper attack.

The German radar and the infrared heat seekers did not function well in attempts to locate the Night Witches flying their Po-2s. Radar did not bounce off the wood and canvas aircraft, it was simply absorbed, so no blip for recognition appeared on the radar screen. The infrared heat seekers were also inefficient in locating the Po-2s because very little heat emissions were emitted from the tiny 110-hp engines. German pilots had to find another way to identify and eliminate them.

The job was delegated to a few of the Luftwaffe's top fighter aces. By using radio communications between the pilot and the searchlight operators, the Po-2s were first spotted and held in the searchlight's beams. Their positions were then relayed to the fighter pilot who positioned himself for the attack. Utilizing this strategy was how the four Night Witches were attacked that lethal night.

The Messerschmitt pilot who attacked the Night Witches that fateful night was Sergeant Josef Kociok, a twenty-five year old Luftwaffe fighter ace. Hitler had promised any Luftwaffe pilot who shot down a Night Witch would be awarded the coveted Iron Cross. He had a total of two hundred day and night combat missions with thirty-three recorded victories (kills) of which twenty-one were at night. That number included the four Witches' planes in one night. He received his Iron Cross as promised, unfortunately he was killed a month later when his fighter collided with a crashing Soviet bomber. While attempting to bail out of his plane, his parachute became entangled and did not open.

Not long after that attack/loss, a few of the Night Witches' planes were armed with a machine gun. The gun was bolted onto the cockpit framework behind the navigator and pointed backwards which gave the navigator an additional duty. The machine gun added weight which then decreased the number of bombs that could be carried. When the newer Po-2s were available with the higher horsepower engine, the machine gun and bomb carrying ability were less of a weight problem.

The regiment moved on as directed by the Soviet Air Force. They had been stationed on the Southern, Trans-Caucasus, North Caucasus, Ukraine, and Belorussian fronts and assisted in the siege of Leningrad in January 1944. The Soviets were gaining strength over the Germans as the Red Army pushed them further and further back toward Berlin.

The Soviets began producing needed war supplies at an unprecedented pace in 1944. Guns, tanks, ammunition, bombs, and aircraft were delivered to the front lines as fast as they came off the production lines. Tanks were updated with armor so thick the German weapons could not penetrate them. One thousand tanks per month were moved into positions along strategic battle fronts.

Aircraft utilized by the Soviet Air Force as well as the Night Witches' little Po-2s were also updated. The new Po-2A model was given a larger 115 horsepower engine, a machine gun, and some even had armor plates in the pilot and navigator's seat backs.

With larger engines, the planes could carry heavier bombs. Instead of carrying four smaller weight bombs, they were then able to carry two larger bombs for missions with larger targets. With the machine gun and its ordinance, the Witches might not have carried any bombs, instead utilized the machine gun to protect the others on the mission from any surprise attacks from the Messerschmitts.

More parachutes were also available; however, the Witches figured since they flew at tree top level most of the time, the parachutes would be useless. They did not carry or wear them unless they knew they would be flying at higher altitudes such as reconnaissance flights during the daytime.

The Soviet forces unleashed what would be its greatest victory over the German occupation of Soviet territories on June 22, 1944. Dubbed Operation Bagration, the Night Witches were there in force.

Just days prior to the Operation Bagration attack, Soviet partisans positioned themselves behind or around the scattered German rear encampments. They started small fires to signal the Witches where to drop their bombs. The Night Witches proceeded to bomb the German encampments, their supply lines, their communication lines, and kept the soldiers awake throughout the night. Together the partisans and the Night Witches scored forty thousand incidents effectively disabling the German rearguard before the main offensive even began on June 22.

For the scheduled strike, the Red Army with 1,670,300 personnel, 5,818 tanks, and 7,790 aircraft from four Air Force regiments, including the Night Witches, spread themselves out over four major German occupied positions. The Germans struggled with only 1,036,760 combat personnel, 800 tanks, and 1,300 aircraft. Since the German supply lines had been cut earlier by the Night Witches and partisans, their ammunition, fuel, and food were extremely limited. They were also battle weary from the Night Witches continuous, nightly harassment bombing.

Operation Bagration was over by August 19, 1944. History records this as the greatest Soviet victory of the Great Patriotic War. Over 50,000 more German prisoners were taken from areas near Minsk alone, and many more in other areas. The Operation covered four hundred and fifty miles and pushed the German forces out of Soviet cities and villages they had occupied. The Red Army was then within striking distance of Berlin.

The devastation and destruction from Operation Bagration was enormous for both sides. German casualties: 450,000 killed or wounded with 262,929 captured or missing. Soviet casualties: 770,888 killed, wounded, or missing. Included in the Soviet casualties were several Night Witches.

As the Soviets pushed into Poland, the Night Witches followed doing what they did best. The largest number of missions flown by the Night Witches in one location were those flown in an effort to liberate Poland.

Next came the suburbs of Berlin in mid-April 1945. The Soviets, along with their allied forces, gradually encircled Berlin. Rumors quickly circulated that Adolf Hitler had swallowed a cyanide capsule then shot himself in the head on April 30, 1945 (*conspiracy theorists say he faked his death and escaped to Argentina where he lived to the age of 95*). Following the announcement of his reported death, German military leaders continued to defend Berlin with fierce fighting ongoing for several weeks. The Germans were completely overwhelmed and finally surrendered on

May 2, 1945. Soviet soldiers climbed over rubble and what

remained of the German Reich-stag (Parliament) building in the heart of Berlin to hoist the Soviet flag. The Fall of Berlin, May 2, 1945 was officially declared the end of war in Europe. Victory in Europe Day—VE Day—was formally declared to the world May 8, 1945.

Soviet flag hoisted over Berlin.

The Night Witches had com-pleted their last bombing mission the night before the surrender. Most were sleeping at their abandoned farmhouse quarters when one of the regiment mechanics burst in shouting, "The war is over!"

The war was indeed over for the Night Witches. The units were officially disbanded October 15, 1945. The Witches had flown 23,672 missions in 1,100 nights of combat from 1941 to the end of the war in 1945, dropped over 23,000 tons of bombs, advanced more than 1,300 miles from Stalingrad to Berlin, and became the most high-ly decorated regiment in the entire Soviet Air Force. Each pilot had flown an average of eight hundred bombing or support missions *(American pilots were rotated out of com-bat flying and sent home when and if they survived twenty five missions)*. Twenty-three Witches were awarded the Gold Star of the Hero of the Soviet Union as well as numerous other awards; five HSU awards given posthumously. Two women were fighter aces. Sadly, fifty lost their lives performing their duties.

Author's note: The Soviets did not publish accurate statistics of wartime women's casualties most likely due to the fact they did not want it widely known they were utilizing women in combat roles with some killed in action. In addition to the Night Witches, there were women infantry, sniper, and sharp shooters who were also killed. Following the war, several of the Night Witches compiled and recorded their experiences. From their histories, this author has utilized their figures as more accurate and truthful.

Some of the Witches continued to fly, a couple became test pilots or went to work in aircraft factories. Many of them simply wanted to return to their families, or what was left of them, and begin rebuilding their beloved Motherland. They did not consider themselves heroes but described their wartime experiences as the most exciting time of their lives. All became lifelong friends and agreed to get together annually.

Only a few books and memoirs were written about these women following the war even though they were the most famous aerial combat unit on the Soviet Eastern Front. They have been quietly forgotten and are little-known today, especially in the United States.

The Free French pilots of the Normandie-Niemen Fighter Regiment (all male) often flew and fought alongside the Night Witches and dedicated the following tribute to them:

"Even if it were possible to gather and place at your feet all the flowers on earth, this would not constitute sufficient tribute to your valor."

Chapter 13

Meet the Night Witches

It would be nearly impossible to write about each of the hundreds of women of the 46th Taman Guards Night Bomber Aviation Regiment, aka the 588th, aka the Night Witches. Instead, this author has chosen a select few to give the reader a clearer picture of these amazing women and their accomplishments. Several of the women discussed here were not members of the 46th Taman Guards but served in one of Marina Raskova's other two units. Their contributions also need to be recognized. Regardless of which regiment the women were in, they considered themselves *sestry,* sisters forever.

Several pilots from the
famed 588th.

Valentina Grizudobova

Before her famous Rodina flight with Marina Raskova and Polina Osipenko, Valentina had already logged 5,000 hours of flight time in a variety of aircraft. She had also set seven world flight records for altitude, speed, and distance.

 Valentina, the daughter of an aircraft inventor and designer, was born in Kharkiv (now Ukraine). At the age of fourteen, she soloed in a glider. She was well educated, played the piano and spoke several languages. At the age of twenty she graduated from the Penza Flying Club of the Osoaviakhim, continued her flight training and became a flight instructor.

When Marina began searching for qualified pilots for her women's regiments, she tried in vain to get Valentina to take command of one of them. Valentina declined the offer multiple times telling her friend she did not want to become a member of an all woman regiment. Instead, she was appointed as the only woman Commanding Officer of a wing of Soviet airmen, the 101st Long-Range Air Regiment. The regiment was formed much earlier in the war from experienced civilian aviation pilots and totaled over three hundred male navigators, engineers, and ground crew. They flew the Lisunov Li-2, a transport aircraft with bomber capabilities but better suited as a supply plane. It was utilized later in the war to supply troops and partisans desperate for ammunition and food. The Lisunov Li-2 required a crew of six: pilot, co-pilot, navigator, flight-technician, radio operator, and gunner.

The Soviet Li-2 aircraft.

Author's note: The history of this plane is interesting and needs to be shared here. Boris Lisunov, a Soviet aeronautical engineer, visited the Douglas Aircraft Company in the United States from November 1936 to April 1939 to learn the specifications of the popular Douglas DC-3 and translate the design for Soviet production. The DC-3 was initially used in the U.S. for carrying civilian passengers and cargo prior to WWII then modified for military use. It was then re-designated a C-47, but lovingly called the Gooney Bird, and used extensively by the U.S. during WWII. The Soviets modified the design to suit their civilian needs dubbing it the PS-84, then modified designs again for military needs just prior to the German invasion and re-named it the Lisunov Li-2. Machine guns were added, bomb racks installed, and doors widened for cargo loading. It was a workhorse of a plane for the Soviets just as it was for the Americans.

Once organized, Valentina's regiment flew day and night, long-range bombing missions over the South and Western Fronts. She flew more than two hundred bombing missions as pilot-in-command (more than any of her male regiment pilots). Some of the most dangerous missions were those flown into the German blockaded Leningrad in June 1942. Heavy anti-aircraft fire riddled the aircraft with bullet holes as her team delivered supplies, ammunition, and food to the starving Red Army soldiers. For her regiment's vital role assisting in the break-up of the siege of Leningrad, they were awarded the honorific "Guards" title in May 1944, thus becoming the 31rst Krasnoselsky Guards Bomber Regiment. The entire regiment was individually awarded the Order of the Red Banner.

In September 1942, Valentina's regiment was assigned assistance to the Partisan Movement.

Author's note: Soviet partisans played an important behind the scenes roll in The Great Patriotic War. Initially, conflicting sources stated that members of the resistance were groups coordinated and controlled by the Soviet government utilizing Red Army hierarchy and tactics. Others stated that the partisans created and organized their own resistance groups. Most agree the partisans were villagers and peasants who came together to fight the German invaders in order to maintain their Motherland's way of life, not necessarily for the Soviet government or its political leaders.

In the spring of 1942, the Central Headquarters of the Partisan Movement was organized and established liaison networks with the Red Army covering various areas of the Soviet Republics. Partisan members included women as well as men, each with a well-defined objective: disruption of the German advance into the Soviet Union. By the end of 1941, over 90,000 men and women had joined partisan forces; 220,000 in 1942; 550,000 in 1943. The partisans secretly gathered information about German troop movements, size, armaments, etc. then reported their findings to nearby Red Army forces. They also printed leaflets and periodic newspapers debunking propaganda broadcasts or newspaper articles originating from Moscow, then distributed them through their underground networks.

Partisans effectively destroyed German supply lines and also assisted the Night Witches. They lit small signal fires, even just a lit cigarette waving in the air, to indicate directions or as a mission marker. The partisans also rescued Night Witches who had crashed, who were injured, and needed assistance to escape their aircraft and return to base. If the pilot and navigator were found dead in their aircraft, the partisans quickly buried them nearby before the Germans found them and desecrated their remains. Any identification papers or belongings were turned over to nearby Red Army officials with a description of where the remains were buried.

As in any war, there are often bad guys mixed with the good guys. Some partisans stole food, farm animals, cloth-

ing and looted from locals who were barely surviving them-selves. Many partisans were captured by the Germans, tor-tured for information then either sent to German POW camps, labor camps, or killed on the spot.

Women partisans also faced high risks as they primarily worked the underground networks assisting refugees, Jews, and children in ways of escape, food, and clothing needs. The partisan women's greatest fear was to be captured by the Nazi Germans, raped, tortured or sent to labor camps, work farms, factories, or the feared Ravensbruck, the brutal women's concentration camp near Berlin.

Valentina personally led her regiment on more than 1,850 missions to provide partisans with over 1,500 tons of arms, ammunition, radio equipment, a printing press, paper, food, and medical supplies. They evacuated 2,500 wounded partisans to field hospitals as well as hundreds of young, homeless orphans to safe areas.

Following the war, Valentina continued to fly and worked in civil aviation. She became Chief of Flight Test-ing at the Scientific Research Institute of Civil Aviation. She was appointed by the Supreme Soviet of the U.S.S.R. as the only woman to serve with nine men on the "Ex-traordinary State Commission For Ascertaining And Inves-tigating Crimes Perpetrated By The German-Fascist In-vaders And Their Accomplices, And The Damage Inflicted By Them On Citizens, Collective Farms, Social Organiza-tions, State Enterprises And Institutions Of The

<u>U.S.S.R."</u> *(the actual full title of the commission!)*. Findings and reports from this commission were utilized to prosecute Nazis at the Nuremberg Trials.

Besides her Rodina flight award, Hero of the Soviet Union, she received a long list of other awards and was highly regarded as a Soviet war hero. She retired from the military in 1946, married an army pilot, had a son and lived quietly with her family. Valentina Grizodubova died in Moscow April 28, 1993 at the age of 83. A monument honoring her achievements is located in Moscow.

Monument honoring Grizodubova

Lydia Litvyak

Lydia Litviak or Lilya Litvyak *(alternate spelling most referred to her as Lilya)* was a sassy bleached blonde, petite, a bit shy at first, quiet, thoughtful, mischievous young

woman, who was deadly serious about her flying. Born in Moscow August 18, 1921 to Jewish parents, Lilya grew up in a small home near the subway station. Her father was a railroad worker, her mother worked in a store near their home. Her father was executed by the Stalin regime during the Purge in the late 1930s; deemed an "enemy of the people" along with millions of others. These were meaningless deaths to the government but cruel, heartless murders to their loved ones. Lilya made it her life's personal mission to clear his name, as he had done nothing wrong as a civil servant.

Everything about aviation intrigued her from an early age. Her favorite book at the age of twelve featured the biographies of Americans Orville and Wilbur Wright. She read the small book over and over until it began to fall apart then tied it together with string. She enrolled in an Osaoviakhim flying club as soon as she was allowed. She studied aircraft design, navigation and meteorology on her own and fell in love with aerobatics. At the age of fifteen, with just four hours of flight instruction, Lilya soloed in a Po-2 trainer plane. Soon thereafter, Lilya graduated from the Kherson Military Flight School and became a flight instructor at the Kalinin Air Club. When the Great Patriotic War began she had already trained forty-five pilots who quickly enlisted in the Red Air Force. She was still a teenager, just eighteen!

Lilya answered Marina Raskova's call for women pilots in October 1941, and arrived at Engels for training along with the other volunteers. The first problem with Lilya, and encountered by all concerned, was the humiliation of the required hair cut; she flat out refused to have her hair cut. She held out for two days, finally relenting after a convincing chat from her idol, Marina. Lilya was very particular about her hair. After it grew out following the buzz cut, she kept it fairly short and bleached it blondish-white with peroxide (she obtained the precious liquid from nearby field hospitals whenever her regiment was close to one). Later on during her service, after her last mission of the day

Lilya (standing) perhaps after washing her hair?

or night, she drained the hot water from her plane's radiator into a bucket, added a bit of cold water if it was too hot, then poured the water over her head, lathered with soap, then rinsed. Lilya then wrapped her head in a well-worn towel and retreated to her quarters only to re-appear a short time later with a dry head, hair shining and bouncy clean!

Her stubbornness and defiance became her trademark and served her well as she moved on at Engels.

Yak-1 fighter

Lilya made it crystal clear to Marina throughout training at Engels that she wanted to become a fighter pilot assigned to a fighter regiment. She proved her flying skills with every flight in the Yak-1 fighter planes and was duly assigned to the 586th Fighter Regiment by Marina.

Those chosen for the 586th received their first assignment May 18, 1942, and was the first regiment to leave Engels. Their mission was to defend the munitions plants and railroads from the Germans at Saratov. It was a fairly easy assignment in which all the pilots gained flight time and fighter experience. From that first fighter mission, she established her trademark return to home base; Lilya buzzed the airfield with a low level, fast pass, pulling up sharply, gained altitude, then did a couple aerobatic loops or rolls. Although reprimanded each time, as long as she did not have her flying privileges taken away or sent to the brig, she just smiled, shrugged her shoulders and muttered, "It's my signature for a mission accomplished!"

In September Lilya and Katya Budanova, her best friend and fellow fighter pilot, were transferred to the all-male 73rd Fighter Regiment near Stalingrad where the fighting was furious in the air and on the ground. Although the regimental commander was desperate for more fighter pilots, he was dismayed at the arrival of the two young women with their support crews. "We're waiting for real pilots and they sent us a bunch of girls," he lamented. His disapproval carried over to the male pilots who refused to fly a plane serviced by a female mechanic or fly the same plane after a woman pilot had completed her missions. All of them soon ate their words!

On September 13, Lilya's first day of flight over Stalingrad, she scored her first two aerial victories, one of which was a highly regarded German fighter ace, Erwin Meier. Meier was flying a Messerschmitt escorting German bombers when his group was attacked by the Soviet fighters. An aerial dogfight ensued between Meier and Lilya, with Meier looking for his lucky thirteenth victory of a Soviet plane. It didn't happen. Lilya struck the Messerschmitt with her 20-mm cannon rounds sending it plummeting to earth. Meier abandoned his ship and parachuted into Soviet held territory. As he floated downward, Lilya circled him twice, gave him a little wing wave and salute, then flew off for more action.

When the Soviet troops captured him, he wanted to meet the man who outflew him; after all, he had been awarded the Iron Cross because of his ace status twice - an ace pilot has scored five aerial victories or kills - and thought he was indestructible. Back at the airfield he was introduced to a small, teenage girl with shocking blonde/white hair who could speak limited German. He laughed and told them they were playing a joke on him - he wanted to meet the "man" who had shot him out of the sky. Lilya proceeded to describe every detail of her dogfight with him as she looked him squarely in the eyes, smiled coyly, then saluted him and walked away (probably to go wash her hair after the mission). Her legendary status began at that moment.

She became the first woman in history to shoot down an enemy aircraft in air-to-air combat. The next day Lilya scored her third victory; a shared victory with Katya Budanova. After just two days flying with her new unit, the regiment commander had to digest his earlier words regarding the female pilots.

Author's note: Earlier Soviet history books report Valeria Khomiakova was the first woman to down an enemy plane in combat. Newer information and statistics released after the fall of the Soviet Union in the 1990s compare dates and recognize Lilya Litvyak as the first woman rather than Valeria by eleven days. The newer information also clarified that Valeria's victory was a night victory. The newer information also confirms the first woman fighter pilot killed during the Stalingrad action was Klavdya Nechayeva who was attacked by a German Messerschmitt.

Lilya continued to reek havoc with the Germans over Stalingrad. She loved flowers and often picked a handful before each mission and placed them in her cockpit, pinned them to her uniform, or scattered them over the aircraft wings before takeoff. One day she asked her mechanic to paint a large white lily on each side of the fuselage near the tail of her plane. This may have been a bad idea. The Germans now had an identifier for the ace woman pilot. Thinking the painted white lily was actually a rose, they began calling Lilya "the white rose of Stalingrad," which was a nicer moniker than "the she devil in a dark green killing machine." The Germans also placed a bounty on her; anyone killing her would receive the coveted German Iron Cross from Hitler himself.

In October 1942, Lilya, Katya and two other women pilots were sent to the elite 9th Guards Fighter Aviation Regiment, often referred to as the "Regiment of Aces." This regiment was being reorganized as a unit with skilled, aggressive pilots in possession of ace status or close to it. This was a combined men and women's unit without harassment between the sexes. It was a group with mutual respect and admiration for each other and the individual accomplishments each had achieved. This regiment also became a turning point or milestone in recognizing the strength of women as elite fighter pilots during the war.

Lilya's fighter victories continued through the winter and into the New Year with an additional six victories (three German fighters and three transports). She was awarded the Order of the Red Star in February and advanced in rank to Junior Lieutenant. She was also selected to begin flight missions as an *okhotniki* or free hunter (pilots who search for targets on their own and attack them).

Between Lilya's daytime fighter regiment and the Night Witches, the Germans were losing their attempt to occupy Stalingrad.

After she shot down a German bomber on March 22, 1943, she was attacked, hit and suffered a large shrapnel wound to the upper leg. She tied her scarf, tourniquet style, around her leg and continued to fight. She shot down a Messerschmitt adding another two victories in one day to her score. Returning to her airfield, she landed safely even though in severe pain and bleeding heavily from her wound. When her crew approached the aircraft, they immediately noted her ashen color. She was losing consciousness due to the heavy loss of blood that had pooled on the floor of her aircraft. Crewmen rushed to lift her gently from the cockpit and called for a medical transport. She was sent to a field hospital for immediate treatment then on to Moscow for further care and recuperation.

The injury left her with a marked limp and persistent pain. She spent her recuperation time visiting her mother and brother at their home, which was miraculously still standing in Moscow, then returned to her regiment in May.

Upon her return, she was anxious to get back into the sky right away. Her Commander was hesitant to allow her to fly due to the obvious limp and her attempt to cover and hide her pain. She insisted, persisted, and finally wore him down. She volunteered to take out a German observation balloon that was targeting Soviet infantry and destroying their supplies, thereby rendering them unable to advance. Other fighter pilots had not been successful in eliminating the balloon.

The hydrogen filled balloon was tethered in an open field near the village of Troitskoye about ten miles behind the front line. The balloon was attached to a wench that was used to let it up to a certain height or pull it back down to

Tethered observation balloon.

the ground. A small basket was suspended under the balloon where the observer tracked enemy activity, troop movements, artillery, etc. then passed the information to his superiors on the ground. At the base of balloon operations was a large circle of heavy anti-aircraft artillery all pointing toward the front line, ready for any frontal attack.

After gathering intel from previous failed attempts to destroy the balloon, Lilya planned her attack carefully. She took off in her fighter plane and flew directly into enemy territory at tree top level away from the balloon. Then she abruptly reversed course and dove to a level of less than one hundred feet from the ground. With the sun at her back to blind any observers, she took aim at the balloon from about five hundred yards behind it. All the ground forces and their artillery were pointed in the opposite direction, caught completely off guard and totally surprised. The balloon was struck by her machine gun then exploded immediately into a huge fireball that could be seen for miles. The Soviet troops, not far from the site, were cheering wildly and waving as she flew over their encampment giving them a low level fast pass, an aerobatic roll and a wing waggle - a pilot's way of saying hello.

On June 13, 1943, Lilya was appointed Flight Commander of her Squadron. She scored and shared another victory on July 16, but her fighter plane was hit and badly damaged. She made it back to base but had to make a wheels-up, belly landing which caused her bumps, bruises, and minor lacerations. She refused to take another lengthy medical leave, fearful she would not be allowed to continue flying. On July 19 and again on July 21 she shot down two more bombers. The flight on the 21st was another dogfight with a German ace. She sustained flesh wounds to her leg and shoulder while her plane suffered major failures; she crash landed in enemy territory but was quickly picked up by a fellow pilot just as German troops approached to capture her. Again, she refused medical leave after simple first aid treatment.

In the meantime, three of her nearest and dearest friends and fellow fighter pilots, including Katya Budanova, were killed within two weeks of each other. Lilya was devastated, then angry. She began flying with a blood thirsty vengeance, even more so than before.

The early morning of August 1, 1943, dawned hot and humid. At her base near Krasnyy Luch in Donbass, Ukraine, the inside of Lilya's cockpit was already sweltering as she climbed aboard and strapped in. She had four missions to fly that day beginning with a fighter escort of Soviet bombers over German held positions. Along with fellow pilots, they tangled with two Messerschmitts scoring a victory for her and a shared with another. Lilya returned to base for fuel and a small bite to eat before returning to the sky for her fourth mission of the day. Her squadron of six Yaks went hunting for German bombers reportedly headed their way. High in the sky were big, puffy, white cumulus clouds that were great for hiding in. All fighter pilots were on the lookout for surprise German attacks. They did not have to wait long.

Thirty German bombers, with twelve fighter planes escorting them, dropped from the clouds like a flock of angry birds. Lilya and her squadron were totally outnumbered as the Messerschmitts attacked them to protect their bombers. It was a deadly aerial circus with eighteen fighter planes dogfighting each other. Lilya and her squadron tried sideslipping, rolls, 200 m.p.h. dives and split second maneuvers in an all-out effort to evade the high powered Messerschmitts. At one point Lilya had two German fighters diving and shooting at her tail. Her plane was hit multiple times but she continued her efforts to out maneuver them. She dove into the clouds for cover for just a few seconds then was seen diving directly at her two pursuers in what was known as the *sokolinyudar*, the falcon blow or ramming attack, a last ditch effort flight maneuver, almost suicidal. Then she was gone. Vanished into a big puffy cloud. There was no explosion, no falling, flaming aircraft or debris, no parachute, nothing. Gone. She just disappeared without a trace over German held territory. She was seventeen days away from her twenty-second birthday.

An extensive search for Lilya and her aircraft by both Soviets and Germans turned up nothing. The German pilots helped in the search because they wanted to confirm the kill for the Iron Cross award. Lilya was recommended for a posthumous Hero of the Soviet Union award; however, the request was denied because there was no proof she was actually dead. Instead, she was declared MIA (missing in action).

The latest military statistics released in the 1990s indicate Lilya Litvak completed two hundred and sixty-eight missions, scored fourteen solo kills, six shared kills, plus the balloon. One of her former regiment commanders, Major Boris Eremin called her "a born fighter pilot." She was the highest scoring woman ace of all time in the world, and the most successful female fighter pilot of WWII.

Lilya's strange disappearance without a trace was likened to Amelia Earhart's disappearance in 1937. Earhart's mystery continues to be well-known and searched for while Lilya's mystery has simply faded away. Both women were great aviation heroines. Like Amelia's disappearance, the rumors about Lilya surfaced quickly and continue to be disputed to this day.

In 1979, the human skeleton of a woman pilot was unearthed near the small village of Dmytrivka. The remains were of a small sized woman in a flight suit with gold fillings in her teeth which seemingly fit the description of Lilya. The skull appeared to have had a mortal wound. No identity papers were found with the remains. Pieces of a Yak fighter plane were found nearby offering more definitive proof that this was, indeed, the long-sought after crash site of Lilya. These details were presented to officials at the Soviet Ministry of Defense, accepted as sufficient evidence of her death (KIA, killed in action) and her records were changed.

Political bureaucracy moves at a snail's pace in any country; it took from 1979 to 1986 to effect that change. Four years later, on May 5, 1990 during the celebration of the forty-fifth anniversary of the Soviet Union's victory in the Great Patriotic War, Mikhail Gorbachev awarded Lilya a posthumous Hero of the Soviet Union medal, presenting it to her brother Yuri. It was one of the last HSU awards given before the collapse of the Soviet Union in 1991.

The mystery was once again brought to public attention in 2004 after Ekaterina Polunia, the chief mechanic for the 586th, published her memoir. In it she described multiple reports that Lilya had been pulled from her crashed plane by German soldiers, marched off the field and subsequently sent to a German prisoner-of-war camp where she was held until the war ended.

The curator of the Litvyak museum in Krasnyi Luch, Valentina Vaschenko, has vehemently disputed Polunia's claim. She stated the female remains found near the village of Dmytrivka were examined by forensic specialists and confirmed to be those of Lilya Litvyak. She related villagers' stories passed along about local partisans finding Lilya dead in her cockpit. They quickly buried her in a trench before German soldiers arrived to desecrate her remains.

An academic authority on Soviet women in combat during the Great Patriotic War, Dr. Kazimiera Jean Cottam, studied the evidence Polunia presented in her memoir. She compared it with other documented facts, conducted her own interviews, and concluded that Lilya did not die as a result of her crash nor had remains matching Lilya's description ever been recovered or positively identified. One source Dr. Cottam sited is a report from a fellow fighter pilot of Lilya's, Vladimir Lavrinenkov, who stated he had personally seen Lilya in a German POW camp where he had also been held.

Another interesting report brought to light by Dr. Cottam was a television program broadcast in 2000 from Switzerland. The feature was an interview with a former Soviet woman who was a fighter pilot during WWII. The woman claimed to have been wounded twice in combat. After the war she married, had three children and was currently (at the time of the broadcast) living abroad. One of the former Night Witches, Nina Raspopova, saw the television program and recognized the woman as Lilya Litvyak. Lilya would have been 79 years old in 2000 during that television interview.

In 2013, Gian Piero Milanetti published his book, *Soviet Airwomen of the Great Patriotic War.* In his discussion of Lilya Litvyak he sites a witnessed report of an "airwoman" parachuting from a disabled aircraft near the location of her disappearance. No other women Soviet pilots were reported to have been in the area which was heavily occupied by German troops. He believes she was captured by Germans, sent to a POW camp then emigrated to Switzerland when released at the end of the war.

Perhaps Lilya was reminded of the brutality of the Soviet regime under Stalin. Her father was executed for no good reason and had always weighed heavily on her mind. Red Army and Air Force personnel were well aware of Stalin's Order Number 270: "No Soviet soldier was to surrender, they were to fight to the last; anyone captured by the enemy would be considered a malicious deserter, a traitor, shot on the spot if returned to the Soviet Union and family members subject to arrest." Stalin said, "There are no Soviet prisoners of war, only traitors."

If, in fact, Lilya was captured by the Germans, she knew she could not return to her mother and brother nor could she let them know she was alive. She would be shot as a traitor and her family sent to prison or worse. Maybe she did what she could with what she had and what she knew?

Lilya Litvyk definitely earned her place in history. A monument was placed in her honor near the airfield from where she last flew at Krasny Luch. The Lilya Litvyk museum is also located there.

This small, simple gravestone marks the supposed burial site of bones thought to be those of Lilya Litvyk. It is located in the middle of a barren open field near the tiny village of Marinovka.

Yekaterina Budanova

Yekaterina Budanova, Katya to her family and friends, was born December 6, 1916 to a poor peasant family in the  village of Konoplanka in Smolensk Oblast. She was tall for her age, short brown hair, average appearance, high marks in school. She loved music from an early age and had a beautiful singing voice. She was always smiling and cheerful, often using her beautiful voice to cheer others with a lively song. When her father suddenly died, Katya quit school and began working as a nanny to help support the family. Her mother sent her to Moscow when she turned thirteen to live with her older sister. Together the sisters worked as carpenters in an aircraft factory where Katya was first introduced to aviation. Like so many other children her age, she enrolled in an Osaoviakhim flying club, learned to parachute, fly gliders, trainers, then received her pilot's license in 1934 at the age of eighteen. She received her flight instructor rating three years later. Katya flew a Yak-UT-1, a single-seat trainer, and participated in several "air parades;" Americans called them flying circuses at that time, then later called them air shows.

When the Germans attacked in 1941, Katya answered Marina Raskova's call for women pilots and found herself at Engels with the other volunteer recruits. Engels was where she and Lilya Litvyak became the best of friends. Although Katya was five years older than Lilya, their lives seemed closely entwined: both had lost their fathers, both were highly skilled pilots, both had a love of their country, and both encouraged Raskova to appoint them to a fighter squadron. Katya joined Lilya as a fighter pilot in the 586th and each flew their first mission in Yak-1 aircraft on May 18, 1942.

The two pilots had the same aggressive flight skills often flying together on assigned missions or apart as wingmen to other pilots. Katya scored her first kill the day after Lilya scored her first, then the two shared a kill the following day in fierce fighting over Stalingrad. Katya was also promoted to the 9th Guards Fighter Regiment of Aces at the same time as Lilya. Each continued to score aggressive kills along with the highly regarded respect of the male fighter pilots in their regiment. Katya was awarded the Order of the Red Star for personal courage and bravery in battle at the same time Lilya received hers. The two were also promoted to Junior Lieutenant at the same time. Katya was also selected as a "free hunter" along with Lilya.

When Lilya was sent to Moscow in March 1943, for surgery and recovery from her leg wound, Katya accompanied her per orders from the Regimental Commander. While in Moscow, the two women were interviewed by *Ogonek,* a political-literary (propaganda) weekly type of magazine for young adults. The magazine cover photo was of Katya and Lilya. The article featured the detailed account of their accomplishments as women fighter pilots which, in turn inferred by the article, honored the Soviet regime. Both women felt they were fighting for their Motherland, not the Soviet regime. The women were not overly happy about the article's inference and downplayed it as best they could.

While in Moscow, Katya also visited the aircraft factory where she had previously worked and talked with her former co-workers about some of her exploits as a combat pilot. At some point during this time period *(unclear to this author the exact time/date due to conflicting information)*, Katya learned that her mother and sister had been killed in an earlier air attack on Moscow by the Germans. Katya became an orphan with no remaining family. Lilya and their regiment of fighter pilots then became her only family.

Katya and Lilya scored the majority of their combat kills while members of the Regiment of Aces. Combat flying was dangerous and demanding for all of the pilots, especially keeping Stalingrad from being overtaken by the Germans. The Germans were averaging six hundred to eight hundred combat/bombing flights a day from August through October 1942, according to Soviet sources. The Red Air Force regiments struck them relentlessly day and night in their efforts to wear the Germans down. Katya and Lilya, with their ability to "free hunt" along with other ace pilots, played an important role in keeping the Germans at bay while increasing their own combat kills.

On July 19, 1943, Katya and Lilya prepared for their early morning mission to escort bombers from near Novokrasnovka. It was hot and humid, typical weather for that region and time of year. Shortly after takeoff and flying in escort formation, the two ace pilots spotted three Messerschmitts bearing down on the Soviet bombers. They immediately went into action in an effort to keep the German fighters away from the bombers. An aerial dogfight ensued with Lilya knocking out one of the Messerschmitts. Katya positioned herself behind the second German plane and opened fire, knocking him out of the fight. One more Messerschmitt left. Katya pulled her fighter plane straight up into the air searching the sky for the lone Messerschmitt. When she spotted it, she dove down after him firing as she went. Another aerial dogfight began, although short lived. The Messerschmitt fired at Katya then turned back with heavy black smoke and a sputtering engine.

Katya and her plane had also been hit. As flames began racing up the wings, heavy, choking smoke filled her cockpit. She was able to put the flames out by some tricky aerial maneuvers which also cleared some of the smoke, then spotted an open field to make an emergency landing. Although the field looked smooth from above, it was full of trenches and foxholes. The landing gear collapsed when it hit a deep trench causing the aircraft to flip over and burn.

Nearby villagers had witnessed the dogfight in the air then watched as the plane rolled inverted, flipped back over and began its spiraling descent to earth trailing thick black smoke. Although they rushed to the site of the overturned and burning aircraft, they were too late. They pulled Katya's lifeless body from the wreckage and buried her a short distance from Novokrasnovka. She was twenty-seven years old.

Katya Budanova flew two hundred sixty-six aerial combat missions in just one year of combat fighting. There is conflicting data regarding Katya's aerial victories. One source lists a total of eleven kills with six being individual and five shared. Others claim she had a total of eleven individual and five shared. Still another claims she may have had as many as twenty total, but unconfirmed. With either number and the fact she was killed in action she would have been entitled to the Hero of the Soviet Union award. She did not receive the HSU at the time of her death for whatever unknown reasons. Along with her other awards she received the Order of the Patriotic War twice.

On October 1, 1993, fifty years after she was killed in action, Ekaterina (Katya) Budanova was posthumously awarded the Hero of the Russian Federation by Decree of the President of Russia, Boris Yeltsin. The street in Moscow where she lived prior to the war was renamed in her honor and a memorial was established at her former high school.

Both Lilya and Katya proved to the world that women could be fighter pilot aces. Both women are recognized, to this day, as the world's two greatest female fighter aces during WWII. Sadly, the history books of today bear little, if any, mention of these remarkable young women and their amazing accomplishments.

Nadezhda Popova

Nadezhda Popova *(alternate common spelling Nadia or Nadya)* was perhaps the most outspoken young lady of the famed 588th, later the 46th Taman Guards Night Bombing  Regiment, the Night Witches. Born in Shabanovka, Ukraine December 17, 1921 near the coal fields, she was the first daughter of a hardworking railroad man. She was cute, perky, loved to sing and dance with a longing to become an actress or a doctor. She did well in school, participated in school plays and musicals, and always stayed busy to keep boredom at bay. One day she watched, with utter fascination and awe, as a small airplane landed near her village. A tall, handsome pilot climbed down from the plane and greeted the crowd that had quickly gathered. A bit bewildered and apparently lost, he looked at the surroundings then asked the crowd for the name of their village. After being told, he smiled, waved to the gathering, then climbed back into the cockpit and took off into the bright blue sky. That plane was the most amazing and fascinating thing she had ever seen. Forget becoming an actress or a doctor, Nadia wanted to fly an airplane! She immediately began to explore aviation from that time forward.

First, Nadia tried to enroll in a flight school at the age of fifteen, without her parent's consent; the school rejected her application. Undaunted, she appealed to Polina Ospipenko, the Inspector for Aviation in the Moscow Military District, who reviewed her paperwork then sent a recommendation to the flight school. She was accepted into the Kherson Flight School and immediately began her flight instruction (still without parental consent or knowledge!). Her first solo flight and first parachute jump were accomplished at the age of sixteen with her official pilot's license earned a short time later. She graduated from flight school at the age of eighteen and became a flight instructor in the Ukraine.

When the Great Patriotic War swept like a violent storm over the country, her family was immediately grieved. Her only brother Leonid, aged twenty, was killed as he fought on the front line in the early days of the attack. When the Germans invaded her family home, they occupied it as a Gestapo police station where they interrogated and tortured Soviet citizens for a variety of misconstrued reasons or charges. She also witnessed grinning German pilots diving their planes and shooting at fleeing Soviet women, children, the elderly, and disabled. It sickened and angered her. She volunteered for duty as a military pilot; unfortunately, Marina Raskova had not yet formed her regiments of women pilots and crew. At that time the military would only accept women as nurses, communications operators, or anti-aircraft gunners. None of those positions appealed to her - it was piloting or nothing; so she waited for the right moment to come along.

When Raskova's call went out for volunteers, Nadia was one of the first to register. She met Raskova for a personal interview and was accepted on the spot.

In October 1941, just nineteen years old, Nadia boarded the train with the other volunteer recruits and headed to Engels for training. After training was completed and regiment assignments were made, Marina appointed Nadia as flight commander of one of the squadrons in the 588th.

On that fateful training night of March 10, 1942, mentioned earlier, it was Nadia who led her squadron on a practice bombing mission. It was snowing heavily when they took off which reduced visibility and increased disorientation. Two of the three planes became separated from Nadia. One plane reportedly became lost, ran out of fuel and crashed, the other plane also crashed possibly due to disorientation in the heavy snowfall. Two pilots and their navigators were killed that night.

Because Nadia was the flight commander, she was initially blamed by her superiors for the two plane crashes. She was devastated by the loss of her friends, even more by the accusation of fault. Upon further review of the incident and witness reports, it was determined the heavy snow disoriented the other two pilots. They were unable to determine up from down, then consequently flew straight into the ground from an altitude of approximately 2,000 feet. It was ruled a tragic accident due in part to the Po-2 aircraft lacking advanced instrumentation.

Early on the morning of May 23, 1942, the 588th launched their regiment from Engels to the Southern front in the Ukraine, Nadia's home territory. They were ready to begin their bombing missions and anxious about the unknown, the unexpected. From the book *Flying for Her Country* by Amy Goodpaster Strebe, comes a quote from Nadia as she recalled her first actual combat mission:

"It was a very, very dark night. Not one small star could be seen. The sky was covered in cloud; it seemed that it was an abyss of darkness, marked by green, red and white tracer lights, where skirmishes continued throughout the night. I followed the lights towards the accumulation of enemy troops. Suddenly, the plane in front of mine got caught in three and later five projector lights, which blind pilots. I watched them fall to the earth right in front of my eyes and saw the explosion of flames below. I flew towards the enemy lines, thinking I must help my friends. Irrational thoughts...I knew they were dead. We dropped the bombs on the dots of light below. They shot at us and I circled round and flew back towards the base. When I landed I could see they already knew. I was ordered to fly another mission immediately. It was the best thing to keep me from thinking about it."

After her first combat mission, when she did have "time to think about it," she realized she had witnessed eight of her fellow comrades-in-arms die over a short period of time. Her regiment was just getting started on the front line; how long would this go on? How many more of her regimental sisters would die? Would she die? It was this reality check that turned her thoughts of joyous flight time to the seriousness of each and every mission. Concentration had to be clearly focused on nothing but each mission, the flight leader, and the target. Fear became an unwelcome copilot for Nadia as well as the others. Another quote by Nadia from *Flying for Her Country:*

"We were frightened all the time. You didn't think about it during the flight, but later. We flew each night, and all through those years never slept enough. There was an enormous strain on the nerves. I would see images of burning planes crashing with my girlfriends in them whenever I closed my eyes. I hoped that if my time came it would be an instantaneous death. The thought of being severely disfigured scared me much more. I was young and pretty, and I wanted all the things every young girl wants. I wanted to live a life I would not be ashamed of if I survived."

Miraculously, Nadia did survive. Her friends told her she was born under a lucky star. Before each mission she would pin her lucky charm, a beetle brooch, to her flight suit. Although she was shot down several times, escaped her burning aircraft a couple of times, made a few emergency landings, she was never wounded seriously enough to prevent her from flying her next mission.

Nadia loved flying the Po-2 plane. Because of its maneuverability and its ability to fly low and slow, she credits the little plane for her ability to escape the fast German Messerschmitts. Since all of the Night Witches learned to fly in these planes, they were used to not having the sophisticated instruments available in the newer aircraft.

For each mission, the pilot and navigator carried a map, a compass, and a stop watch. Just prior to take off, the maps were carefully reviewed, the bomb sites marked, and the calculations of air miles and time to drop site were figured. Using the stop watch and compass, the women knew how long to fly and in which direction to drop their bomb payload. A small flashlight in the cockpit was a rare luxury for checking the map or stopwatch; otherwise, it was pitch black on moonless nights.

In several postwar interviews Nadia recalls a few of her favorite missions. Some were not bombing missions but humanitarian aid missions to Soviet Army and Navy troops or partisans.

In late 1942, while her regiment was stationed just outside Novorossijsk near the Black Sea, her regiment commander received an urgent request from the Navy. A naval squadron occupied a small section of the city on the seacoast and had been cut off by the Germans. They had no water, ammunition, medical supplies, or food. Some of the sailors were injured and all were in need of urgent assistance.

Nadia and her navigator were assigned the mission. They had to fly over German held territory in order to reach the sailors and drop the needed supplies. There was no place to land as there was dense forest on one side and the seashore on the other. Nadia flew over the Germans at an altitude of about 3,000 feet to avoid anti-aircraft fire. She then dropped quickly to near tree shaving level, looking for an open space along the seashore to drop her cargo of supplies. Suddenly, her navigator shrieked "watch out for the towers!" So intent on watching the seashore, Nadia failed to see the towering buildings just ahead and had to take immediate evasive action to avoid crashing into them.

They dropped the supplies just as the Germans fired up their anti-aircraft guns aimed in their direction. Shells whizzed by them and into the aircraft from all directions. Nadia dropped to an altitude of just over three hundred feet out over the sea, out of reach of the anti-aircraft guns, then maneuvered her way back to the airfield.

Back on the ground she found forty-two bullet holes in the wings, her map holder and her helmet. Luckily the wings did not catch fire and no bullet got past her thick leather helmet into her even thicker skull. The commander informed her of a radio message received from the sailors acknowledging they had the supplies and were grateful for the effort.

After the war, Nadia was honored in her hometown and asked to tell a story or two about her war experiences. After she told the above story to those gathered, a young man quickly approached her, nearly knocked her over to give her a big, heartfelt hug and with tears in his eyes told her she had saved his life. He was one of the sailors in that stranded unit. They thought their unit was doomed to starvation and capture by the Germans. They were terrified of being sent to a German POW camp. When the Germans opened fire on her plane, the sailors never knew if she had made it safely back to her base. He hugged her several more times with tears falling, kissed her on both cheeks, and with a big smile on his face walked away, turning once to wave at her.

The other story Nadia fondly recalls took place on August 2, 1942 near Cherkessk. She was assigned to a daytime reconnaissance mission; recon missions did not require a navigator so Nadia was flying alone. She was surprised and attacked by German fighter planes. After being shot down and forced to land, she quickly escaped from her burning plane and made her way to a large group of Soviet troops and partisans nearby. Uninjured, her plan was to walk back to her base or catch a ride from a partisan and continue her missions.

There was an injured Soviet fighter pilot in the group by the name of Semyon Kharlamov. He was handsome, even though disheveled, dirty, and heavily bandaged. What caught Nadia's eye about this young airman was when the group stopped to rest he would pull out a book and read. The book was *And Quiet Flows the Don* by Mikhail Sholokhov, an epic Soviet novel of the time. Nadia and Semyon struck up a conversation and shared flight experiences. From then on, they would see each other various times, off and on, until the war ended. The two found each other in Berlin when the war ended and inscribed their names in pencil on the Reichstag building.

When Nadia's regiment reached Poland, the Axis forces had begun their retreat. The Soviet fighters and the Night Witches fought day and night to maintain their ground and pushed the Germans to continue their retreat. The Germans were desperate and did not want to be defeated, but the Soviets and their allies pushed them hard. It was while fighting in Poland that Nadia flew an astounding record of eighteen missions in one night.

By the end of the Great Patriotic War, Nadia's record was flawless. At the age of twenty-four, with three years of service, she had completed eight-hundred fifty-two missions and received the coveted Hero of the Soviet Union medal. She also received the following awards: Order of Lenin, Order of the Red Banner, Order of the Patriotic War 1st class, twice, Order of the Patriotic War 2nd class, Order of the Badge of Honor, and the Order of Friendship. She retired her lucky charm, the beetle brooch, and proudly wore all of her awards, ribbons and medals to any and all formal functions.

When she returned to her hometown, she received a hero's welcome including a marching band, flowers, and two thousand cheering citizens. Nadia married that handsome blue-eyed wounded fighter pilot who continued on in the Soviet Air Force and attained the rank of Colonel. Semyon Kharlamov also earned a Hero of the Soviet Union award for his wartime efforts. When the two Heroes of the Soviet Union married, they became quite a rarity. They were blessed with a son, Aleksandr, who followed in the footsteps of his parents by graduating from the Air Academy and becoming a General in the Belarussian Air Force.

Nadia worked as a flight instructor for nearly twenty years before finally retiring. She was always upbeat and enjoyed speaking to individuals or groups regaling them with war stories of the Night Witches, of which she was so proud to have been a part. She would always remark about the courage, comradeship, and self-sacrifice of the women who were "just doing their jobs."

Her husband died in 1990. Nadia died on July 8, 2013 at the age of 91 in Moscow; she was the last surviving, original Night Witch pilot.

"Sometimes, on a dark night, I will stand outside my house and peer into the sky, the wind tugging at my hair. I stare into the blackness and I close my eyes, and I imagine myself once more a young girl, up there in my little bomber. And I ask myself, 'Nadia—how did you do it?'"

Indeed Nadia, how did you do it?

Alexandrovna Timofeyeva-Yegorova

Better and simply known as Anna Yegorova, born September 23, 1916 in the small village of Volodova, north

west of Moscow, Anna became another Soviet combat hero during the Great Patriotic War.

One of sixteen children, Anna came from a poor peasant family. Her father served in WWI and in the Russian civil war. He died at the age of forty-nine as a result of health difficulties incurred during those war years. Due to her family circumstances Anna learned about survival from an early age. She studied history and physics in school then moved to Moscow at the age of sixteen where she began work for the *Mosmetrostroy,* the Moscow Metro Construction Department, building the underground transit system. The company had an aero club which she eagerly joined and where she learned to fly.

Anna was accepted into the Ulyanovsk flight school at the age of eighteen but was soon expelled after her brother was innocently arrested as an "enemy of the people." Working a series of odd jobs to survive (bookkeeper, locksmith, and tutor at the aero club) she was finally accepted into the Kherson Flying School and graduated in 1939. She was then hired as a flight instructor at the Kalinin municipal aero club.

When the Germans launched their initial attack on the Soviet Union in June 1941, Anna was among the first to volunteer as a pilot for front line service. The Soviet Red Army Air Force signed her up on the spot and sent her to the 130th Air Liaison Squadron, an all male unit. This was not one of Marina Raskova's groups; her three groups had not yet been formed.

Anna's duties in the 130th Squadron were considered combat missions since she flew dangerous reconnaissance in broad daylight at low altitudes over German infested territories. She scouted their troop movements, encampments, tank and artillery numbers, then reported her observations to her superiors. She also flew wounded soldiers and doctors to field hospitals, delivered mail and important messages, photographed and mapped routes, searched for stranded regiments in remote areas, dropped supplies, transported military officials, government officials, and war correspondents.

All missions were flown in the little Po-2. Anna called it her "tireless workhorse." Through sunshine, blue skies, rain, sleet, snow and ice, she boasted, the Po-2 did not fail her. Unless, of course, the "Fascist Hawks," as she called the Germans, shot her down.

On May 20, 1942, Anna was dispatched to deliver an urgent secret message to the front lines where frantic, fierce fighting was taking place (the Second Battle of Kharkov). She also carried a large bag of mail, most likely headed for Soviet troops in the area. On her way, she was attacked by a

Messerschmitt that set her Po-2 on fire. As mentioned earlier, the Po-2s were flying match boxes and Anna knew she had to escape before being burned alive. Because of her altitude, she could not bail out (altitude to high) or jump without a parachute (altitude to low). The cockpit was quickly filling with acrid, blinding and choking smoke, while flames danced and raced across the wings toward her. She put the plane into a steep dive and headed toward a large cornfield she spotted below. The tall, withering corn was surrounded on one side by a lush, green forest and a small village on the other side.

The Messerschmitt continued to shoot at her as she miraculously crash landed the plane into the corn. On the ground, she quickly secured the package with the secret messages inside her flight suit then jumped from her burning plane. In her haste to avoid the growing flames and choking from the thick smoke, she left the large heavy mail sack on the bottom of the cockpit along with her favorite leather flight jacket. The Messerschmitt's machine gun continued to strafe her as she stumbled among the tall cornstalks. The bullets struck the corn and dirt around her as she dropped to the ground in an attempt to hide. The burning plane sent a thick plume of black smoke into the air as Anna continued to run through the tall cornstalks headed toward the forest to hide. Finally, the Messerschmitt turned away, seemly satisfied he had added another Soviet "kill" to his belt by destroying the plane.

Anna then headed toward the village she spotted while in the air. She needed to get the package to the 9th Army Headquarters and knew it was somewhere close to the village. She heard a large truck rumbling down the road and tried to flag it down. It drove around her, as did a car not far behind the truck. Fuming, she drew her pistol and fired a shot into the air after the car passed by. The car braked suddenly leaving a long skid mark, then quickly backed up to where she was standing in the middle of the road, smoking gun in hand.

The car had military officials inside en route to the 9th Army Headquarters. Anna showed her identification papers, explained her mission and what happened. All the men starred at her for a few seconds in disbelief then quickly made room for her in the car. She was quite a sight to see with her hair singed in places and stuck with cornstalk pieces, flight suit burned, dirty and tattered, her face, arms and hands sporting bright red burns, dirt splotches, bloody cuts and scrapes. She sat silently with her head held high as the military car sped on. Upon arrival at Headquarters she promptly delivered her package with the secret messages, was patched up by the medics, and was returned to her base.

During her one year of service with the 130th Squadron she flew two hundred and thirty-six missions and was awarded the Order of the Red Banner twice for distinguished service. But she wanted more. She wanted to fly real fighter combat missions and she wanted revenge on the German Fascist Hawks.

She was transferred to the 805th Attack Aviation Regiment, an all male unit, where she was quickly trained to fly and fight in the Illyushin Sturmovik Il-2 air-to-ground attack aircraft. Little did Anna know that Marina Raskova had sent multiple messages to the 805th Commander requesting she be transferred to Marina's 587th Bomber Regiment. The Commander would not let her go, nor did he let Anna know of the multiple requests until after the war.

The Il-2 was a single engine, propeller-driven, low-wing monoplane specifically designed for assault operations. It was fast, had armor plating to protect the plane, pilot, and

The Illyushin Sturmovik Il-2

gunner, machine guns for aerial combat, or bombs and rockets for ground attacks. The Soviet soldiers called it the "Hunchback" or the "Flying Tank," the Germans called it "Black Death." The Il-2 successfully targeted tanks, bombers, and transport aircraft as well as railways, airfields and ships.

The 805th was called upon to assist in a joint mission along the Blue Line. The objective was to lay a smoke screen of sorts to disorient the Germans so the Soviets could advance troops and penetrate the German defenses in the area. The Night Witches had attacked the German encampments a couple of nights before, destroyed a large number of their four hundred supply wagons, and kept the soldiers awake through the night. This aided in the chaos and confusion the next day when the 805th dropped the smoke screen.

Pilots and crew prepared themselves and their Il-2s for the risky smoke mission. The planes were disarmed, then large balloons filled with smoke gas were attached to the bomb racks. The squadron was instructed to fly nineteen

Soviet soldiers advance toward German positions under cover of the smoke screen.

miles in a straight line, aerial formation, across the length of the Blue Line. At the given drop zone, on a timed command, the smoke gas was released and formed a smokey curtain allowing the Soviet soldiers to advance. The Germans fired their anti-aircraft guns blindly through the smoke at the Il-2s, struck several but caused only minor damage.

Anna counted several bullet strike marks all over her plane when she and the others returned to base. All the pilots that flew this successful mission were awarded the Order of the Red Banner when they landed.

"Tonight We Fly!"

Lieutenant Anna Yegorova, the only woman pilot in the 805th, was soon appointed leader of her squadron of male pilots. Squadron leaders often flew the lead aircraft into battle. The Germans always tried to down the lead plane in hopes that the rest of the formation would disengage and return to base. Hopefully, her appointment as squadron leader was not a sign the men wished her ill will.

On the fateful day of August 20, 1944, at the age of 28, Anna lead her squadron of fifteen aircraft along with another squadron, on a mission to attack German forces at the Magnuszew bridgehead near Warsaw, Poland. Once over German territory, anti-aircraft guns began firing relentlessly at the two squadrons. Anna's Il-2 took three direct hits from the powerful guns which thrust her aircraft upwards into the sky and out of control. Her gunner was dead, instruments and radio destroyed, engine on fire. Once again, she experienced her aircraft on fire with her trapped inside it. Flames from the engine were burning through the wall into the cockpit heating her boots, smoldering through her flight suit pant-legs and licking at her legs; she had to get out!

The canopy was jammed and would not open even with her frantic efforts. Her eyes and throat were burning from the black smoke filling the cockpit, her boots and flight suit pant-legs were now on fire. The plane began shaking violently, nosed over, began spiraling to earth, and exploded.

Anna lost consciousness just as the plane exploded. She was thrown clear of the fireball, her body hurtled through the air. She regained consciousness as she was falling to the ground and frantically grabbed for the parachute rip-chord. It was a futile effort. She was too close to the ground for the chute to open completely and it was also on fire.

With a violent, sickening THUD Anna hit the ground and immediately lost consciousness again. It was probably a blessing as she had broken nearly every bone in her body including her back, all of her ribs, crushed pelvis, broken leg, and both arms. Her hands were crushed and her skull was fractured. Her legs and feet were severely burned, hair burned off in patches, and her boots melted to her feet. Nearby German infantry soldiers rushed to her crumpled, lifeless body, not to aid her, but to capture her.

Unable to breathe and in horrific pain, Anna slowly regained consciousness. A soldier had his big filthy boot on her chest shouting at her in rapid German. She could not move or draw a deep breath. Even though a surge of adrenalin raced through her mangled body, she was completely paralyzed by the thought of being taken prisoner by the ruthless Germans. She could not reach her pistol to shoot herself; it had already been taken by her captors. The soldiers tried to pick her up, but her broken bones and back would not support her. She just crumpled back to the ground out of their grasp, screaming and crying out in excruciating pain, then passed out again.

In and out of consciousness for several days, she was finally lucid enough to realize she was in the German POW camp, Kustrin. The Germans had poured a powder of some sort on the burns to her legs and feet which caused her to scream out in agonizing pain for hours on end. Many of the other prisoners caused such a fuss about the young girl's screams, thinking the captors were torturing her, the Germans finally hosed the substance off of her and everyone settled down. The German plan for her captivity was to give her no medical care, food or water. Because she was a woman pilot they assumed she was one of the Night Witches. Their torture plan for her was simply to throw her in a cell to die a slow, agonizing death from all of her injuries and starvation.

One of the prisoners was a captured Russian doctor, Georgy Sinyakov, who pleaded with the Germans to allow him to treat Anna. After several days in a filthy cell, with no food or water, lying in her own excrement, her burns and wounds were now grossly infected, she was feverish and near death. The only other woman prisoner in the camp was a former medical instructor, Yulia Krashchenko, who remained by Anna's side trying to care and comfort her. Between the two, as well as the other prisoners, they did the best they could to keep her alive. Morsels of food from the other prisoners were slipped to Yulia who then fed the weakened Anna. Rain water was collected for her to drink. Encouraging words from Yulia and Dr. Sinyakov helped Anna regain tiny bits of strength, but her broken bones and wounds could not be mended or healed properly without decent medical care. There was no such thing.

Back at the 805th airbase, her returning squadron pilots reported Anna had been shot down, her plane had exploded, and she was presumed dead. Her mother was notified that Anna had been killed in action and she would begin receiving a survivors pension. Anna had flown two hundred and forty-three missions for the 805th and was posthumously granted the award of Hero of the Soviet Union, presented to her mother. Little did any of them know, she was still alive - barely.

On January 31, 1945, after five long, terrifying months in the POW camp, Soviet tanks burst through the walls and liberated the prisoners. When they found Anna, the only woman in the camp (Yulia had been shot to death earlier for disobeying an order from the German captors), the Soviet soldiers assumed she was a traitor or spy and turned her over to the NKVD (Soviet secret police). They in turn sent her to a SMERSH (*Smert Shipionam* or Death to Spies) Soviet prison where only the suspected hard core German prisoners were held, interrogated and tortured.

Anna was interrogated continuously day and night for nine days before the physical torture was scheduled to begin. She received little food or water during this process. She was accused of "being captured," called a traitor and a "Fascist bitch" over and over again. Instead of wearing her down, her interrogators only succeeded in building a rage within her that increased every day of the brutal interrogations. It did not matter that Anna's service records were impeccable and showed she had been a highly decorated officer. She had been stripped of all honors and awards, including the Hero of the Soviet Union which she was not even aware she had been awarded. Perhaps the lowest blow came with the notification from the government that since she was alive, she would be expected to repay all the survivor's benefits that had been sent to her mother, effective immediately, even though she was still being held by the NKVD. It was also obvious that she had sustained horrific injuries that left her with improperly healed bones, barely able to walk, burn scars on her face, feet, and over her body. She needed medical attention.

Authors note: As mentioned earlier with Lilya Lityvk's situation, Stalin and his Order 270 law were such that any Soviets who allowed themselves to be captured alive by the enemy were deemed traitors and subject to arrest, imprisonment, and/or death upon their return home. Their family members would also be subject to arrest, separation, imprisonment, and sent to labor camps. All liberated Soviet POWs were arrested on suspicion of being traitors or deserters. They were deprived of all rights and sent to the SMERSH at Lansberg to be "tested." The testing was continuous night and day interrogation and confrontation with little food, water, or toilet access. Physical torture began after many days of interrogations. Thousands of Soviets succumbed or were shot at the hands of their own countrymen during this imprisonment and torture under Stalin's Order.

On the tenth day of her imprisonment, that rage within had built to an explosive level. When a guard opened her cell door she surprised him by knocking him off his feet then charged up the stairs at a very labored pace to the major's office, threw open the door, stepped onto the plush carpeting and shouted, "When are you going to stop tormenting me? Kill me if you like, but I won't let you torment me any more," then promptly collapsed to the floor unconscious as guards rushed in after her.

Anna was finally released shortly thereafter and returned home. She learned from her mother that she had been posthumously awarded the HSU. Her mother learned from Anna that all her awards had been stripped from her by the NKVD. After a short rest Anna returned to her former regiment where she served until the war ended. She was not allowed to fly due to her ongoing medical conditions, but found other work to assist her regiment.

After the war Anna Yegorova married Vyacheslav Timofeev, her former regimental Commander. She returned to college and received her Masters degree in history as well as technical science, then worked as a high school teacher for many years.

Doctors also told her she should never have children due to the deformities of her spine and pelvis. Despite the dire warnings from doctors, Anna and her husband had two sons, Pyotr and Igor.

On May 7, 1965, after a long and courageous battle with the government, Anna was notified that all her medals, including the Hero of the Soviet Union award, had finally been reinstated and would be returned to her.

She completed her memoir, *Red Sky, Black Death - A Soviet Woman Pilot's Memoir of the Eastern Front*, in 1992.

Lieutenant Anna Alexandrovna Timofeyeva-Yegorova died October 29, 2009 at the age of 93.

Irina Sebrova

Lieutenant Irina Sebrova was born on a cold snowy Christmas day, December 25, 1914 in Tetyakovka, Novomoskovsk. She took her place as the sixth child in a working class family. After she completed her primary educa-

tion, Irina moved to Moscow and enrolled in a trade school where she studied technical courses, nursing, and gunnery. After graduation, she worked for four years in a nearby factory that made boxes for the postal service. One of the factory supervisors took up a collection from all the workers in order to purchase an airplane that would be donated to a local flying club. Four factory workers were chosen to take free flight lessons at the club as a token of appreciation for the donation of the plane. Irina was thrilled to be one of the workers chosen.

Because of this opportunity, Irina found her love of flight and the freedom it presented her. She worked hard with her lessons and quickly accrued flight time in the trainer plane. She went on to the Kherson Flying School, graduated with a diploma and her official pilot's license in 1940, then was hired as a flight instructor. By the time the Germans attacked the Soviets, Irina had taught more than fifty pilots.

Irina answered Marina Raskova's call for women pilots and joined the other recruits at Engels. She was the oldest recruit at age twenty-seven; the majority of the young women were still in their late teens. When studies were completed at Engels, Irina was assigned to the 588th Night Witches and headed for the front-line activities in Ukraine.

As mentioned earlier, the first combat flight for the 588th suffered the loss of four of its members and devastated the regimental survivors. Many realized the seriousness of what they were doing as well as the fragile nature of life. Though stunned by their losses, the regiment continued their nightly missions of harassment bombing along the front lines in various locations where they were needed the most. Regiment members were exhausted all the time from lack of adequate sleep. They flew bombing missions at night and relocated their own bases during the day. More than three straight, uninterrupted hours of sleep was considered a luxury for pilots and crew.

In an interview after the war, Irina recalled one base in the Grozny area of the Northern Caucasus. The bedraggled villagers greeted the 588th regiment with open arms. They were very frightened of the German advancement toward their village after hearing stories of the brutality and ruthlessness of the Nazis; they begged the regiment to stay as long as they could. Most of the villagers were women and children or elderly, not fit to join the Red Army. The regiment remained in that location for six months. The Night Witches protected the village and its inhabitants by bombing the advancing Germans nightly. Although the Germans could not overtake the village itself, they simply rerouted their advancement and went around it instead. This scenario, protecting villages, repeated itself in many of the locations the Night Witches were assigned to protect.

Perhaps the toughest fighting for the Night Witches was along the infamous Blue Line on the Kerch Peninsula. Irina recalled the fierceness of the Germans and the great numbers of large, well-fortified military encampments along the Line. The Germans also had night fighters specifically assigned to hunting the Night Witches. So between their night fighters, search lights, the heavy anti-aircraft guns and ground fire, Irina says the Night Witches had to think fast, take evasive action and be able to maneuver their aircraft quickly to get in, drop their bombs, and get out.

Hampering their efforts during these successful missions was the smoke. Irina recalled the smoke that always filled the air from fires after the bombs hit their mark. After multiple strikes the smoke became thicker as it quietly invaded the open cockpit planes. It caused her and her navigator's eyes to burn and tear, blinding both of them as well as causing them to cough and choke, as they gasped for clean air.

Irina and other pilots remember some of their first bombing missions and how their bodies responded. After the last bomb had been dropped, the extreme tension experienced by the pilots during the mission often caused their bodies to begin shaking uncontrollably all over. Irina described the shaking was like a severe shiver from the cold or hard chills before a fever. The shaking lasted several minutes and usually stopped by the time they returned to base. This was the body's way of reacting to the sudden spike of adrenaline from the mission followed by the quick let down. Not knowing what was happening to their bodies was a scary experience for these young women.

After a long night of multiple missions it was difficult for many of the pilots and their navigators to fall asleep, especially if they had taken the doctor prescribed "Coca Cola" caffeine pills. Knitting or embroidery would often help them relax enough to fall asleep for a couple of hours.

While fighting on the Kerch Peninsula another fellow pilot, Irina's best friend, was killed. She was struck in the head by a bullet and slumped over dead in the cockpit. Her navigator immediately took the controls, returned to base and successfully landed the plane. The navigator, Irina Kashirina, was also killed a short time later during another skirmish with the Germans.

Irina Sebrova had several close calls flying missions with the Night Witches. During one mission, on the Kerch Peninsula, she and her navigator were shot down over the water. She was able to maneuver the crippled plane back over to solid ground and land in an open field surrounded by barbed wire fencing. Remember, the Witches' missions were flown in the dark of night. How they missed the barbed wire fence was just short of miraculous. The two quickly exited the aircraft fearing fire or further attack from the Germans. Luckily a partisan saw the plane come down and rushed to the site in his old battered car. He asked the two disheveled women if they were injured or needed help. Irina told him they were not injured, just scratched and bruised but they needed help to get back to their base. The generous partisan hustled them into his car and told them he would take them to the nearby ferry run by other partisans in the area. They would have to hurry as the ferry only operated at night, and dawn was fast approaching. Once across the water to the mainland, other partisans would be able to assist them back to their base. They arrived at the ferry just before it was ready to leave and thanked the partisan for his help.

Once aboard the ferry, the two women could not believe their eyes. The small ferry was packed with wounded, dying, or dead Red Army soldiers; the dead had a simple cloth covering their faces and heads. The ferry quietly shuttled them across to the mainland, under cover of darkness, avoiding detection by the nearby Germans. Once across the water, other partisans loaded the soldiers into carts or vehicles then took them to a field hospital for treatment or buried the dead nearby.

Irina and her navigator were still in their flight suits and life vests feeling awkward among the moaning, bleeding mass before them. They held hands with some of the dying and gave encouraging words to the wounded. As dawn began to lighten the sky, the beleaguered ferry touched the mainland shore while a squadron of German planes flew overhead shooting at them. The two women jumped off the ship and ran for cover in trenches dug along the shoreline. They eventually made their way safely back to base where they were greeted by a collective sigh of relief from their regiment sisters.

While in Poland, Irina was flying a nighttime bombing mission over the city of Danzig. The city had been overtaken by the Germans. The Red Army and Air Force were slowly but surely pushing them back. Fighting was fierce. On one of Irina's bombing missions she and her navigator were taking heavy ground and anti-aircraft fire. When bullets or flak struck the canvas wings of the Po-2s, they made a snapping or popping sound. If the bullets were still hot after being fired, the canvas wings would smolder briefly then burst into flames. She heard multiple snaps and pops but luckily saw no smoke or flames and continued on with their mission.

As she approached their bombing target, Irina noticed her oil pressure gauge was nearing the zero mark. She had live bombs under her and needed to drop them before she could return to base or make an emergency landing. The engine did not appear to be overheating so she made the decision to fly on, drop her bombs, then return to base. The bombs hit their intended target as planned, then she needed to turn her Po-2 and head for home base.

Still over German-held territory, with increased enemy fire coming at them, the engine began sputtering as its temperature gradually increased. She did not want to crash in enemy territory. What to do? She climbed the aircraft to an additional 1,300 feet above her original 3,000 feet. When the engine finally quit, Irina turned the plane toward home base then glided down in altitude toward it. But she came up short.

Irina managed to crash-land the plane in a large blacked out area. Flying at night and seeing a large area with no lights or building outlines usually meant a large body of water or a heavily forested area. She feared that the black area might be water. If that were the case, she and her navigator would have to immediately jump out of the plane into the water, but which way to swim? How far?

Luckily, the blacked out area was land and the crash landing did not involve water, just bone jarring bumps across a dry field. The two women quickly climbed out of the plane. Not knowing if they were in friendly or unfriendly territory, the two proceeded in the dark with pistols drawn. First they saw a large pile of hay with two shadowy figures lying at the base of it. Friend or foe? Dead or alive? They quietly moved on. A bit further on, the clip-clop sound of a horse approaching with the dark figure of a man riding it caused a cautionary move behind trees and bushes. The two women waited until the horse and rider passed then ventured forth once again.

They walked on following a dirt road for some time and finally heard the sound of an approaching car. Russian conversation could be heard coming from within the car, so the women flagged it down. The driver told the women he had been dispatched to deliver an emergency message to frontline headquarters and could not take them to their base. He gave them directions back to their base from that location and sped away.

The two exhausted women set off once again as it began to lightly snow. According to what the driver had told them, it was a five mile trek back to their base. The thought of a hot cup of tea or some boiled cabbage soup increased their pace as the cold and snow wrapped icy fingers around them. By the time they reached the base, no further missions were to be flown as dawn was lightening the sky. After reporting to their superiors, a pot of hot tea and a warm bed were certainly welcomed. It had been a long night.

By the end of the Great Patriotic War, Irina Sebrova had accumulated the highest number of missions and hours flown by any other pilot during that time. She had flown 1,008 bombing missions; she had also flown an additional ninety-two non-bombing missions for a total of 1,100 over four years. She was awarded the Hero of the Soviet Union, the Order of Lenin, three Orders of the Red Banner, Order of the Patriotic War, the Red Star and several other medals for service.

After the war, Irina continued to work in the Red Air Force as a test pilot. She flight tested aircraft that had been repaired or restored for return to service. Following a life-threatening crash, Irina retired from the service in 1948. She married, had a daughter, and was hired as a professor at the Moscow Aviation Institute. Irina Sebrova died in Moscow April 5, 2000 at the age of 85.

Irina Rakobolskaya

Irina Vyacheslavovna Rakobolskaya was born December 22, 1919 in the small village of Dankov near Moscow. Her father was a physicist and her mother, a teacher. She

had a younger sister and an older brother who was a doctor. When Irina was eleven years old her father died. Shortly after his death, her mother and siblings moved from Dankov to Moscow. In 1938 Irina entered Moscow University to study physics, poetry, and theater. She had no interest in aviation but, like all students, she was urged to join a flying club where she learned basic aviation terminology and how to parachute.

On June 22, 1941 Irina was studying for a theoretical physics exam with a friend when foreign minister Molotov's solemn voice came over the radio. The room became very quiet as the students listened to the devastating news of the German's attack on their Motherland.

Irina answered Marina Raskova's call for women to be trained as combat pilots and shipped out to Engels with the other recruits. Although she had no previous interest in aviation, she expressed a desire to learn to fly when she was interviewed by Raskova. She was told that since she did not already have a pilot's license, as most of the other women did, and because she was educated, Irina would be trained as a navigator. Pilots, navigators and technical staff positions were first filled by young women who had come from colleges and universities. Engineers and ground crew personnel, with minimal experience, came from factories or working families. All would be trained in military ways first, then receive additional training in their appointed fields.

After the Engels training was completed and assignments were made, Irina found herself appointed as the Deputy Commander of the Crew, Chief of Staff in the 588th Night Witches regiment under the command of Lt. Colonel Bershanskaya. The two women worked well together and developed new, innovative ideas for the betterment of the regiment's assignments in nighttime bombing missions. The 588th regiment had over two hundred women when it was first formed, double that number by war's end, with Bershanskaya and Rakobolskaya as the regimental leaders the entire time.

As described earlier, each pilot had an assigned crew of two, sometimes three, whose jobs were to refuel and rearm the planes between missions. It was Irina who noted the armorers were struggling to load the heavy bombs by themselves thereby slowing the readiness of pilots in launching their next mission.

Irina developed a new plan, which was approved by Commander Bershanskaya and briefly discussed earlier, to group the crews and rotate the duties within the group. After Irina noted how successful the turn-around times increased utilizing the new plan she and Bershanskaya set the new plan in place permanently. The new plan also reduced fatigue and injuries to the crew members and sped up the refueling and rearming process. As each plane landed to refuel and rearm, a crew of five, instead of two or three, immediately proceeded to their assigned duties: mechanics inspected the plane for damages, fuelers refueled and checked the pilot and navigator, and three armorers worked together to load the four bombs, two bombs under each wing. Two women carried the bomb from the supply area and handed it off to the armorer sitting or lying on the ground under the bomb racks, then scurried back to retrieve the next bomb. The bomb lifter pushed the heavy seventy to one hundred pound bomb up over her head and into the rack, set the detonator and made sure the release cable to the cockpit was secure. This process was repeated for a total of four bombs per plane. As dawn approached and missions were completed, the bomb squad had carried and lifted over two to three tons of bombs in one night.

When the plane was refueled, all the bombs loaded and secure, the signal for launch readiness was given to the pilot. She taxied the plane into position for takeoff and watched for the go-ahead signal to launch immediately. Total time on the ground was three to five minutes maximum. The next plane in was directed to an open stand and the process would begin again. Planes usually took off in groups of three but did not return in the same order. The groups of crew were always ready to service them as they returned for a quick turnaround. All of this was done in total darkness, unless there was a bright, full moon.

On rare occasions, the bombs would not release, for any number of reasons, when the pilot or navigator pulled the release cable. Since the bombs were armed, the pilot and navigator could not fly back to base and risk an explosive landing. The navigator would have to climb out of her cockpit behind the pilot, gingerly step out onto the wing, grab the fly wires or struts to hang on to, then either kick the bomb lose or reach down and shove it free. This was done as the pilot continued to fly over enemy territory keeping the aircraft as steady as she could. Once the bomb was free, the navigator carefully and quickly climbed back into her cockpit and resumed her duties as navigator. Back at base, the mechanics were advised of the problem and the cable would be immediately checked before the next flight mission.

One of Irina's responsibilities was to assign the mission launch order each night. There were often quiet murmurs among the pilots and navigators when certain pilots seemed to be given frequent first launch assignments. Those initiating the murmurs thought the advantage would be to boost the number of logged missions for those pilots. In fact, when mission launches were tallied, it clearly made no difference. The women were very competitive and Irina tried to rotate the pilots as best she could to quell the murmurs. In a 1993 interview, Irina was asked why the women were so competitive in counting their missions. Her reply was,

"Out of enthusiasm! In order to prove that we could do anything. We were not content just standing on par with men's regiments. We had to constantly increase the daily number of sorties (missions)."

Seasonal darkness and the close proximity of the enemy played a big role in adding to their mission numbers. Longer nights meant more missions. Each round trip flight took forty-five to fifty minutes or less, so it was easy to accomplish ten to fourteen or more flights per night.

During her interview, Irina was also quoted as saying, "The women flew as well as men, and in many respects better, more emotionally, with imagination. After all, they were not required to serve in the Air Force. It was their free will, and that which is done at the call of the heart is always done better than that which is done out of obligation."

Irina kept a close eye on the returning planes after each mission. Without radios to communicate with their base, pilots had no way of letting the crew know they were injured or the plane was severely damaged. Irina devised a signal to alert the ground crew and others when a pilot/navigator was returning with an emergency. Three flares released in rapid succession on landing approach signaled to the ground crew there was a problem. Mechanics were alerted to the possibility of a damaged plane that might need repair or pulled from service. Medics would be alerted to the possibility of an injured pilot or navigator.

The pilots making an emergency landing tried to land farther away from the main base of operations in case the plane was on fire, might cause a fire, or crash due to mechanical problems. In several incidents the planes crashed and caught fire. Ground crew would rush to the scene and attempt to rescue the pilot and navigator from the burning plane. Sometimes their valiant efforts failed.

Irina was devastated when a plane did not return or when she was given a report that one had been attacked and gone down in flames. The airfield base was usually located close enough to the enemy targets that she could watch her planes on their bombing missions if there was a full moon. When Irina personally witnessed one of her pilots and navigators attacked, their plane afire and falling to earth, she felt helpless and paralyzed with grief. She checked her maps and flight assignments to determine who was dying before her eyes. After the war, Irina reflected, "It was the most grievous torture I endured in the army during the war - to calculate who was dying." Irina always displayed a calm and authoritative demeanor while choking back fear, rage, and anger toward the Germans.

Irina also monitored her regiment's health, especially the pilots and navigators. Because the lack of sleep along with the frequent severe weather, frequent relocations and poor nutrition affected the immune system, the young women developed colds, coughs, even pneumonia and other maladies as well as a variety of major and minor injuries. She relieved them of their duties for one or two days to rest and recover or sent them to a field hospital for treatment.

This always caused a protest by the sick or injured individual as it would affect their flight/mission record numbers.

After several of the pilots and navigators had flown their first missions, Irina noticed the young women landed with severely blood shot eyes or a bloody nose and with complaints of sudden, severe headaches. They also had dark bruises across their chests a few days later. She consulted with doctors at nearby field hospitals to determine what the causes might be. It was a puzzle at first, but after studying the flight techniques the women used, the cause quickly became apparent.

The Night Witches began their missions at or above an altitude of three to four thousand feet. Their planes were open cockpit with only a small windscreen in front of the pilot and navigator. When the pilot cut the engine and proceeded into the steep, fast dive, down toward the target, the pressure was so great on the head and face that the tiny capillaries in the temples and behind the eyes would burst. The pilot and navigator screamed in pain as the vessels burst and caused the sudden piercing headache. The pressure on their bodies from being tightly held by their safety harnesses, while in the steep dive, caused the chest bruises. After the bombs were dropped, the pilot quickly restarted the engine then pulled the aircraft up sharply causing her and her navigator to slam back into their hard seats. The plane then reached treetop level or a bit higher and returned to base. By then, the headache was dissipating, but the whites of their eyes turned bloody red while their noses dripped blood for several minutes. It took several days for the eyes to clear, but since the vision was not impaired, they continued to fly. Painful chest bruises took a bit longer to surface then subside. Recommendations were made by the doctor to adjust the steep, high speed dives on the targets; however, it was left to the pilots as to how they wanted to proceed. Most continued the same pattern; their young bodies gradually overcame the pressures and healed quickly.

Night Witches & their aircraft. Note:
the planes are in a grassy field.

There have been frequent mentions of aerodromes, airfields, and airbases. However, because the Night Witches moved frequently, there were no paved runways or elaborate air terminals; instead, there were open fields, streets, dirt roads, or clearings in wooded areas. As long as the field had the length and width to accommodate landing and takeoff of aircraft, it was considered an aerodrome, airfield or airbase to the regiment. Problems encountered at these types of landing sites were unseen potholes or ditches.

The big round tires on the Po-2s absorbed some of the shock, but the pilot and navigator were often jostled and bounced in their hard wooden seated cockpits, sometimes causing injuries. The risk of an armed bomb being jarred lose during a bumpy takeoff had to be eliminated. Upon arrival at a new landing site/base, Irina carefully inspected the proposed "runway" then assigned a crew to fill the holes and smooth the rough spots if needed before night missions began.

During the rainy season, mud was a major problem for the planes, as well as fuel and supply trucks. The wheels became mired in the mud preventing planes from taking off. Fuel trucks could not drive out to the planes without becoming stuck, while supply trucks stayed on the perimeter of the field. Irina directed the crew members to drag logs or fencing from nearby areas, lay them in long rows across the mud then push the planes onto the logs to launch. The crew hung on to the wings while the pilot raced the engine, then let go when the pilot signaled them to do so. When the plane landed, it landed in the mud and had to be pushed, all 1,698 pounds of it, onto the logs for refueling and rearming. Fuel was carried from the fuel truck to the planes in large heavy cans. Naturally, this made a shambles of the three to five minute turnaround time, but the planes were still able to accomplish their missions.

The rainy season also caused problems in the women's quarters. Trenches or dugouts were used by the women unless a farmhouse or an abandoned building near their base could be utilized. After a heavy rain the trench or dugout would be flooded. It was typical for the women to awaken from a mere two hours of sleep to find their belongings floating around them and their makeshift beds soaked in muddy water. In some locations, Irina encouraged the use of an above ground "lean-to" or tent type of structure, instead of digging a trench or dugout.

Irina worked continuously day and night to have her regiment of two squadrons, later four squadrons, prepared and ready for their nightly assigned missions. She caught an hour or two of sleep when she could. She received daily combat orders from nearby ground army commanders detailing the target, its location, and the number of missions to be flown. If the regiment was not close to the assigned target, the entire unit had to move closer to the location and be settled in, ready to fly, before dark.

Irina also gave the squadron leaders the pre-mission briefing. The latest reconnaissance reports were reviewed, maps updated, targets marked, orders noted, current weather reports checked, and finally, any potential dangers that might be encountered (other than the Germans).

Often the orders were to bomb the German's frontline, especially if they had a large encampment of soldiers. Other times the orders were to attack the rear of the encampment that contained their fuel and supplies. On nights with multiple missions to the same encampment, one squadron might be assigned the front line attack while the other squadron attacked the rear. The majority of missions were strictly nightly harassment bombings to stupefy the Germans from lack of sleep. Their reflexes and accuracy would then be off which gave the Red Army an advantage in overtaking them the during the day.

When an extra navigator was needed for whatever reason, Irina often flew the mission. Her Commander, Bershanskaya, also flew as navigator when needed. Irina flew twenty-three combat missions and Bershanskaya flew thirty-five.

Irina Rakobolskaya was like a proud mother with her regiment of young women. Her favorite slogan was "You are a woman and you should be proud of that!" She also frequently reminded them that "a woman can do anything." One February day in 1943, Irina burst through the door of the bunker where the young women were resting and shouted, "Fall in, fall in!" then stepped back against the open door. Her face was flushed as she tried to contain a big, proud smile as it tried to escape across her face. As the women jumped to attention, General Popov stepped gingerly into the bunker. In his hand he held what looked to be an official government folder. A subtle intake of breath passed down the line as the women stood taller in the presence of the respected General.

"By order of the Supreme Soviet and in recognition of your outstanding service to your country…" He began listing the current record of mission numbers that had been flown, the resultant damage to the enemy and their equipment, concluding with the admirable devotion to duty witnessed by the Supreme Soviet then stated, "I am ordered to announce that the 588th Women's Night Bomber Regiment will from today be given the title of the 46th Guards Regiment."

It was difficult to contain their excitement, enthusiasm, giggles, and murmurs as the General moved down the line and shook each young woman's hand. To be awarded the title Guards Regiment was the greatest collective honor the unit could receive. It also acknowledged the women as an elite fighting unit. Irina's slogan definitely rang true; they were all now, definitely proud to be accomplished women. The 588th was the first unit to receive the coveted Guards distinction and renamed the 46th Guards Night Bomber Aviation Regiment.

In October 1943, it was given the additional title of 46th Taman Guards Night Bomber Aviation Regiment after its participation in the Soviet victory on the Taman Peninsula. Eighteen pilots and six navigators from this unit alone received the honor Hero of the Soviet Union as well as numerous other awards, ribbons, and honors. Sadly, Irina recalled losing thirty members from her regiment alone. With each loss she prayed for a quicker end to the war.

Her prayers were finally answered May 8, 1945 when Germany surrendered. Yuri Levitan, the voice of Radio Moscow, announced, "Attention, this is Moscow. Germany has capitulated...this day, in honor of the victorious Great Patriotic War, is to be a national holiday, a festival of victory." Joseph Stalin later addressed the Soviet people, "My dear fellow countrymen and women. I am proud today to call you my comrades. Your courage has defeated the Nazis. The war is over...now we shall build a Russia fit for heroes and heroines."

Shortly thereafter an official decree was issued by the government to demobilize all Soviet women from military service with few exceptions. Irina's beloved regiment of young women officially disbanded in October 1945.

Irina was the self appointed chronicler of the Night Witches regiment during and after the war. She kept the memory of the women and their achievements alive by publishing diaries, memoirs, giving interviews and organizing the annual reunions.

She met and married her husband, Dimitri Linde a Professor of Radiophysics, in 1946. They had two sons, Andrei (Professor of Physics) and Nikolai (Professor of Psychology).

Irina went back to college and finished her physics degree at Moscow University in 1949. She studied cosmic rays and nuclear physics, authored or co-authored over three hundred academic papers, six books and a textbook on nuclear physics. She accepted the position of Chair of the Physics Department at the University and in 1994 was honored with the lifetime position of Distinguished Professor. In 2013, a documentary on her extraordinary life and unprecedented achievements was broadcast on Russian television.

Irina Rakobolskaya died September 22, 2016 at the age of 96.

Support Crew

The unsung heroes of the 588th Night Witches were, no doubt, the support crew members: mechanics, fuelers, armorers. Without them and their hard work, the pilots and navigators would not have accomplished the high number of missions they scored reeking havoc on the Germans. Pilots and navigators who received the coveted Gold Star Hero of the Soviet Union always shared and acknowledged the honor with their technical staff and mechanics.

Remember, the 588th was the only regiment that was entirely made up of females, including the support crew. Only for one, very short period of time did a male species arrive to help. The shy young man was sent to install an air-to-ground communications system at one of their bases. He kept to himself - even ate his meals alone and away from the young women. When a supply order of women's underwear arrived, his name was also listed due to a misspelling denoting the feminine gender. The poor guy was mortified. The work on the communications system was completed in record time and the young man returned to his own regiment—without that new underwear!

Aircraft mechanics worked night and day to prepare or repair the Po-2s. The little aircraft was easy to work on because it was so simple and basic. Bullet and flak holes in the canvas wings and plywood fuselage were easy and quick to repair; however, too many repairs to the wings reduced the overall integrity of the fabric. Holes in the wood were carefully checked for possible smoldering damage from hot flak. Damaged engines or their parts took longer to repair. Mechanics often had to scavenge parts from severely damaged, unflyable Po-2s. When the loss of an aircraft prevented a mission from being flown, the mechanics worked together to have one available within hours.

As mentioned earlier, there were no luxurious, temperature controlled hangars for the mechanics and crew to work in. Weather and location were always factors that had to be dealt with in accomplishing their duties. Regardless of the conditions, the planes had to be ready every night for their pilots and navigators.

Freezing cold, snowy conditions were the hardest for the crew to work in. Below zero temperatures made it difficult to work on metal parts of the aircraft. The women had to remove their heavy, clumsy gloves to feel the nuts and bolts. In so doing, their fingers stuck to the cold metal then the skin ripped off when they pulled away. At other times, their hands and faces suffered frostbite from exposure to the extreme, below zero air temperatures.

During blizzard conditions with high winds, the light planes were in danger of being pushed away or into other planes parked close by. With nothing to tie the aircraft to, the mechanics laid across the lower wings and hung on for dear life until the storm abated. Although covered in a fine blanket of snow and nearly frozen to death, in most cases, the planes did not wander off and did not sustain damage.

A light snow did not often deter the night flying missions; the crew simply attached skis to the aircraft wheels.

When supply trucks were unable to reach the bases due to impassable roads from the sleet, ice, and snow, critically low levels of food, fuel, and ammunition were reached. A cargo plane would be sent to an accessible location near the regiment where a suitable landing space could accommodate the larger plane. The cargo plane's landing site was relayed to the regiment along with 'come-and-get-it orders.' The regiment commander quickly assigned a few available pilots to retrieve the needed supplies. When the orders were received, the crew collected what little fuel was available from the regiment planes, then filled the tanks of the planes assigned the supply retrieval mission and hoped there was enough for the round trip flight. Only the pilots flew for the supplies in order to save room for the return loads. Once they returned, it was only the crew who unloaded all the supplies but everyone rejoiced at having food, fuel and ammunition once again so flight missions could resume.

Crew members trying to push a supply truck out of the mud.

Spring rains brought mud, mud, and more mud. Trenches filled with water, and dirt roads used as landing strips became impassible for supply trucks as well as airplanes. When an airplane became mired in mud, an empty supply truck was often used to drag it out. That usually resulted in both the truck and the plane completely stuck. Logs and boards found nearby were hauled by the crew to the site then positioned in such a way as to provide traction under the truck tires while the crew worked together to push the truck out of the mud. It was always an all-out effort to rescue the vehicles.

The blistering heat of summer presented crew members with another set of harsh difficulties. Just as the frozen nuts and bolts caused ripped skin, the heated metal caused burns to the fingers while the sun burned exposed skin. Heat sickness was common in areas with high temperatures and humidity, especially when adequate clean water was not available for drinking to maintain hydration.

The women (crew as well as pilots and navigators) often hid their injuries or illnesses for fear of being sent for medical care or ordered to stand down and rest for a few days. As time passed, not reporting their injuries or illness eventually caught up to them. Wounds became infected, frostbitten toes had to be amputated, burns left ugly scars. In one instance, a young woman had severe joint swelling, high fever and unusual fatigue. Her regiment teammates urged her to seek medical help but she refused until one day she became so ill she could not get out of bed or stand up. She was diagnosed with rheumatic fever and spent several months in a hospital recovering then had lifelong residual difficulties. Scarlet fever was also prevalent, and dysentery was a frequent problem when contaminated water was consumed.

In their later years, mechanics and crew suffered severe, crippling arthritis to their hands due to the repetitive fine motor skills used to do their jobs. Scaring on their hands also contributed to the arthritis. Having the skin of their hands repeatedly torn off during freezing conditions or burned in extreme heat, caused the scars. The skin could not heal properly or sufficiently between injuries which then formed the deep scars. Joints and ligaments eventually seized from the scaring and the crippling arthritis set in. Hands constantly in kerosene and oil added to the complications.

Besides weather and medical difficulties, there were also creature difficulties. In the late fall and early winter, rats and mice were everywhere, into everything, including the planes. Mechanics had to frequently repair wiring and cables in the planes after they had been chewed by the rodents. In one instance, a mechanic watched as her assigned pilot and navigator lifted off on a daytime mission. Moments after a successful takeoff the plane suddenly began making strange shaking maneuvers in an awkward, unapproved, wild flight pattern. The pilot immediately turned the aircraft back toward the landing field. She shot off three flares in rapid succession to indicate an emergency landing was necessary. When the plane landed, the two women immediately jumped from their cockpits and ran screaming across the field while batting furiously at their flight suits. Mechanics and crew rushed to the plane. They were somewhat baffled when they could find nothing wrong with the plane after a brief inspection.

One mechanic thought they were on fire as they continued to bat their flight suits, but there were no flames or smoke. Other crew rushed to aid the women as they continued to shriek and scream then began stripping off their suits. Unknown to all concerned, mice had been in the plane when it launched and several had crawled up the women's pant legs! Upon closer examination of both cockpits an entire family of rodents including grandparents, aunts and uncles were found!

Rodents may have been easier to exterminate than mosquitoes. Many of the regiment's encampments were near rivers or lakes which were breeding grounds for mosquitoes. The women were delectable treats for the insects causing itchy grief, swollen faces, arms and legs for everyone. On rare occasions someone would have a bad reaction to more than multiple bites and need to seek medical care.

Each mechanic took her job very seriously. She never wanted a sloppy job to result in the loss of a plane or the death of its pilot and navigator. They were devastated when a plane returned with a pilot or navigator severely wounded or dead from enemy fire. It was the crew's duty to assist them from the aircraft, take them for medical care or bury them nearby.

When a member of the 588th was killed in a crash, the crew members were responsible for digging a grave near the base of operations where the death occurred. A small ceremony was held and wildflowers placed at the site. The grave was marked and a description of the burial site sent to officials who then notified the next of kin. If regiment members were killed in German occupied areas, the partisans or nearby villagers who witnessed the crash tried to retrieve the body or bodies before the Germans could get to the crash site. Depending on the area and circumstances, the partisans would either bury them nearby or attempt to return the bodies to the base. Identification papers and personal affects would be sent to the base, along with directions and descriptions of the burial site. Pilots and navigators gathered the belongings of their *sestry,* sisters, wrote notes to the family, packaged the items carefully, lovingly, then saw that the package was sent to the family as soon as possible.

Armorers also braved the elements of weather and creatures to load the planes with bombs and munitions. During

Armorers preparing to lift bomb into bomb rack.

the day armorers and mechanics carefully examined the bomb racks and cables for signs of damage from the night before. At night the armorers hand carried the bombs from the supply area to each individual plane, one at a time, then handed each off to the armorer(s) stationed under the lower wing(s). The Po-2 wings were so low to the ground that the armorer had to crawl on her knees carrying the seventy to one hundred pound bomb then lift it into the rack. Once the bomb was secure in the rack, she armed it by setting the fuse device. In freezing temperatures, she had to remove her gloves to set the device which invariably caused a loss of skin. Unless there was a bright full moon, the armorers did their jobs in total darkness. Racking and arming the bombs was done entirely by touch and feel.

Armorers quickly built their bicep muscles carrying and lifting the heavy bombs. They were also the quickest to experience increased fatigue, and the dirtiest from having to lay in the mud or snow, dust and dirt to load the bombs. Each night the armorer teams rotated their duties so that one woman was not the only one lifting bombs up into the racks all night long (this was Rakobolskaya's plan discussed earlier).

When machine guns were added later in the war, the armorers had to rearm those as well. Each gun held 270 bullets. The bullets were loaded into a link belt and placed into a metal munitions box until needed. The heavy box was carried out to the aircraft, lifted up onto the wing then into the navigator's cockpit. The link was inserted into the machine gun which made it ready to fire. The ShKAS type of machine guns frequently jammed, usually at the most inopportune moments, but could easily be repaired by the crew or mechanics back at the base.

During the night the aircraft launched in precise intervals of several minutes, remained in formation to their target and returned to base to refuel, rearm then launched again. They did not return in the same precise time intervals in which they had launched, so returns were often unpredictable. Battle damage during the mission or wounds to the aircraft, pilot or navigator slowed the returns. Navigational errors or disorientation in poor weather also caused delayed returns. The ground crew had to be ready for anything as the planes returned one by one. In many cases, there were crashes near the landing site, mid-air collisions, or, in some instances, the plane and its crew did not return at all.

When poor weather reduced visibility, the crew set out kerosene lanterns or lined up available vehicles with their headlights on to indicate the landing site. This was only done after the first wave of planes had dropped their bombs and were headed back to base. The crew surmised the Germans would be too busy recovering from the surprise attacks to go looking for the women's base, so they felt safe placing a few lights to guide the planes in.

Fatigue was ever-present for all involved. The mechanics and armorers worked all night, slept two to three hours, then started their duties again in late morning. It was necessary to exam all the aircraft in daylight for damages, then prepare them for the nightly missions.

At one point during the Great Patriotic War, when nightly missions were highest and most demanding, the 588th worked one hundred days without a break or day off from fighting. For their hard work, the mechanics and crew received a monthly salary of 70 rubles, about $1.08 in U.S. currency today. Pilots and navigators received a bit more.

Mechanics and crew became close to one another as they worked side by side to defeat the Germans and save their Motherland.

One aircraft mechanic, **Inna Pasportnikova**, served in several regiments where she became close to her pilots. She had followed Lilya Litviak as her mechanic for some time when Lilya gave her the nickname "Professor." When news reporters or journalists approached Lilya for interviews, which she did not like to give, she referred them to her professor "…she knows everything." When Lilya was deemed missing in action, Inna helped search for her until the search was called off and she was assigned to another regiment. She was heartbroken, as so many others were, over the loss of Lilya.

When the war ended Inna worked as an aviation engineer with experimental aircraft at the Moscow Aviation Institute for thirty years. All those years between the end of the war and her retirement, Inna agonized over the thought that Lilya had not been found nor awarded a Hero of the Soviet Union; she had died heroically fighting for her Motherland and clearly deserved the honor. According to military regulations the HSU could not be awarded to anyone MIA. When Inna retired in 1976, she joined different group efforts over several years searching for the location of Lilya's remains. Oftentimes her husband and grandchildren joined her in the searches. Although conflicting reports and other arguments persist to this day, *(refer back to the Lilya Litviak section)* Inna and others were successful in having Lilya's records amended to KIA instead of MIA then posthumously awarded the HSU. Inna proudly stated, "That's what sisters do!"

All in all the success of the 588th certainly positioned the regiment for the well-deserved award of Guards unit. The hundreds of young women in this particular regiment worked together from the beginning to the very end as a cohesive team. The Night Witches and their support crew were proud and honored to have become the 46th Taman Guards Night Bomber Aviation Regiment.

Chapter 14

Sunrise for the Witches

Most stories end with the hero or heroines riding off into the sunset and all becomes right with the world. In this book the opposite is true, our heroines flew off into the sunrise, not the sunset. Presaging dawn, the first faint lightening of the eastern sky before sunrise, had been the Witches signal to return to base; their night was done.

When the Germans finally surrendered May 2, 1945 the Witches experienced that presaging dawn. The Battle of Berlin ended that day when German General Helmuth Welding unconditionally surrendered the city to General Vasily Chuikov of the Soviet Red Army. The Witches saw the first rays of sun begin to peek over the horizon as the ink dried on the initial surrender papers. As more German High Command officers signed surrender documents, the final record included the phrase: "All forces under German control to cease active operations at 2301 hours Central European Time on May 8, 1945." With that decree, the Witches finally saw the full glorious sunrise; their night had definitely ended!

Victory in Europe Day, VE-Day, was celebrated throughout Europe while fighting continued to rage on in the Pacific. Victory over Japan Day, VJ-Day, would come August 15, 1945; the official signed surrender took place on September 2, 1945.

For the Soviet military and citizens, the Great Patriotic War was finally over. Four years of death and destruction, along with governmental upheaval, had come to an end. Depending on which leader had control over the release of statistical data and censorship at varying times, the number of deaths reported by the Soviets range anywhere from seven million to forty-three million. The following numbers were compiled averages released after the 1990s *(some sources suggest these numbers are on the low side)*: eighteen million non-military citizens dead; over nine million combat deaths; several million citizens and military personnel died while being held in German POW camps; four million Soviet military missing, presumed dead or deserted. Famine, mass murders of civilians suspected of crimes against the Soviet regime, disease… the list for loss of life causes in the U.S.S.R. alone was long. The Great Patriotic War was the most horrific war in world history. It would take nearly thirty years for the Soviet population to return to pre-war numbers.

Joseph Stalin ordered a Victory Parade to be held in Moscow's Red Square on June 24, 1945. The order read in part: *"...To mark the victory over Germany in the Great Patriotic War, I order a parade of troops of the Army, Navy, and the Moscow Garrison, the Victory parade, on June 24, 1945, at Moscow's Red Square. Marching on parade shall be the combined regiments of all the fronts..."*

Forty thousand Red Army military personnel from all branches marched in the two hour parade along with 1,850 military vehicles, tanks, and artillery. A flyby had been planned, however the weather was overcast and rainy which cancelled the aerial demonstration. The parade was the largest military display in Red Square history.

Ten full crews from the 588th, 46th Taman Guards  Night Bomber Aviation Regiment, with their Commander Bershanskaya, were expected to attend in full dress uniform sporting medals they had been awarded during the war.

Two groups from the 588th in full dress uniforms sporting medals they had been awarded.

Although the war had been declared over, small skirmishes remained ongoing in the furthest outreach areas of the Soviet Union. Communication of the cease fire order was slow in reaching those areas but a welcome relief to both sides when word was finally received.

The process of demobilization of thousands and thousands of military men and women did not happen over night. Thousands of Soviet troops were in Berlin when it fell and had to make their way back to Soviet territory to their respective home bases. The 588th Night Witches were

A portion of the 40,000 military participants in the
Moscow Red Square Victory Parade June 24,1945.

among those stationed in Berlin before, during, and after
the surrender. Members of the 586th were stationed in
Hungary while the 587th was near the Baltic. All three regiments had to move aircraft, personnel and equipment back
to Soviet bases as soon as possible for demobilization.

Women serving in other branches of the Soviet military
were rapidly discharged as soon as they returned to their
home bases. In July 1945, President Mikhail Kalinin spoke
to a large gathering of recently demobilized military
women. His speech was lengthy with undertones of a return
to the old adage "a woman's place is in the home." First he
acknowledged their bravery, sacrifices, and strength in de-
fending the Motherland. Then he underhandedly stated that
the national emergency of war was over, thank you for your
service, keep quiet about what you did, the military no
longer needs or wants you, you are unsuited for combat, go

home. In his closing remarks, President Kalinin stated, in part:

"Equality for women has existed in our country since the very first day of the October Revolution. But you have won equality for women in yet another sphere: in the defense of your country arms in hand. You have won equal rights for women in a field in which they hitherto have not taken such a direct path. But allow me, one grown wise with years, to say to you: do not give yourself airs in your future practical work. Do not talk about the services you rendered, let others do it for you. That will be better."

His speech infuriated the Soviet military women. They were essentially ordered not to talk about their combat experiences, but the men had no such order? Did the military men receive the same speech and directive? No, they did not - another example of the political propaganda regarding the questionable existence of gender equality Soviet citizens had to live by. Women in all branches of the military fought heroically and successfully to defend their Motherland. They expected to be remembered and honored as heroes alongside the men that had done the same jobs. However, the threat of noncompliance to any decree issued by a governmental higher-up was not worth the risk of speaking out or disobeying. The heroism of the women was downplayed due in part to this decree, then lost in history.

Needless to say, the women of Marina's three regiments were happy the Great Patriotic War was finally over and hopeful for a return to normal, whatever that was to be. The majority of the women wanted to continue to fly. Civil aviation jobs were possibilities; however, they would not hire former women fighter pilots because they were thought to be too aggressive! Military flying would be challenging with the newer more powerful aircraft being built. It was thought women pilots would most likely be unable to handle the speed and power. Plus, they would have to be trained. But wouldn't the men have to be trained also?

Medical exams were required for civil aviation jobs as well as the military. Some of the women pilots could not pass the exams for either military or civilian aviation due to residual effects caused by their war duties; improperly healed wounds, lingering infections, breathing difficulties, poor hearing, etc. They received medical discharges from the military and were excluded from civil aviation; thus, their flying days were over forever.

The most common complaint for pilots, navigators, and all crew was extreme fatigue as mentioned throughout this story. All the women were war weary. The majority of these young women were only in their late twenties when the war ended. The continuous, unrelenting stress from their four years of combat service took its toll after the war by manifesting as unrelenting fatigue, frequent headaches, anxiety attacks, and/or the inability to simply relax and fall into a sound, restful sleep. Nightmares were common, even as they grew older; reliving the sight of a fellow sister plummeting to her death in a fireball of a plane or having a plane that had mechanical difficulties and wouldn't fly while loaded with bombs. Some dreams were not always nightmares; reliving the thrill of flying, the companionship of the sisters, or the wishful romance with a handsome young male pilot.

It also took several months to simply get used to sleeping at night instead of just a couple of hours during the daytime. Physicians at that time told the women they were suffering from "battle fatigue" and that they would "get over it soon enough." Today we recognize these symptoms as PTSD, post traumatic stress disorder, and offer a variety of treatments to military personnel to help recognize and overcome it.

Not all of the women from the three regiments wanted to continue flying. Some were happy to return to the studies they had abandoned before the war and finish their degrees in science, engineering or other fields. Many accepted teaching positions at colleges, universities or vocational schools. Besides teaching, other positions filled by military women included chemists, engineers, lawyers, aircraft mechanics, government office workers, physicians, police officers, even positions with the KGB. Several of the women returned to their previous factory positions in textiles, aircraft or machine manufacturing.

Wartime romances resulted in a number of marriages between the military men and women. Those women not pursuing continued flight time or a career were happy to establish a home and start a family. In fact, for a short time the government offered awards to women who gave birth to seven or more children within a given time frame in an effort to rebuild the horrific war losses to the Soviet population.

When the Witches returned to their homes after demobilization, many were devastated to find they no longer had a home nor a family. Their homes had been destroyed by German bombers or taken over then destroyed by German soldiers when they left. Family members were either dead, sent to labor camps, or missing. There was no food anywhere; productive farmland had been desecrated by the Germans or pillaged by starving villagers. It was heartbreaking and surreal. Night Witch pilot Nadia Popova remembered the heartbreaking devastation she and others felt when they arrived home and found nothing. "We came home to face all the destruction and severe food shortages," she told an interviewer. "We worked eighteen hours a day to reconstruct...we didn't have time to reflect on our personal experiences in the war, we were too occupied by the present."

Millions across the U.S.S.R. were homeless and hungry. The government was in turmoil, the economy barely existed and the infrastructure was all but destroyed. Reconstruction plans emphasized heavy industrial output over agricultural food production. That was a big mistake. The citizens were already starving to death, yet the government expected the work product to come above food production. Collectivization was still in affect for the peasants and villagers who were expected to restore the desecrated farmland to productivity. Farmers were shot and killed if found stealing their harvested foodstuffs to feed their starving families before turning their products over to government officials. The government utilized Gulag prisoners and drafted young men for the backbreaking reconstruction of the infrastructure.

Once again, the women were underhandedly called upon to pull the Motherland back together. If not working as teachers, nurses, physicians, or in other professional capacities, the women were called upon to work in the factories. They also maintained their households and did their part to increase the population as mandated by the government. By the end of 1945, over sixty percent of the workforce in Moscow alone was made up of women, many who had previously served in various military positions.

Although the United States was an ally to the Soviet Union during the war, things became cold from 1947 until 1991. The Soviets had opposing economic viewpoints and political ideologies with the U.S. as well as an ongoing competitive nature for their own international political influence. The Soviets also refused assistance from the U.S. via the Marshall Plan; they simply disagreed with the terms and conditions. The Plan was an agreement in which the U.S. pledged to provide $12 billion in aide for European postwar recovery. The Plan would have certainly helped the millions of starving Soviet citizens, but the government remained steadfast in their refusal to accept.

The nuclear arms race between the two countries also caused political problems. This period of time was known as the Cold War between the U.S.S.R. and the U.S.A. A chilliness between the two countries remains to this day.

The Night Witches and all other Soviet military women changed roles once again after the war. From sniper, tank driver, spy, front-line combatant, to dive bomber, or fighter pilot, the women returned to their inherent roles as mothers, wives, and rebuilders of their beloved Motherland. Those inherent roles were forcefully encouraged and lauded by the postwar government while it continued to profess gender equality.

Afterword

After extensive research for this book, I found many examples of Soviet arrogance and propaganda which distorted the historical facts pertaining to the Night Witches. The Soviet government boasted they were the first country in the world to declare legal equality for women beginning in 1917. Yet, what they preached did not follow what they practiced in many cases. There were blatant, underhanded motives, especially during the Stalin regime, that were prime examples. The Osoaviakhim paramilitary organizations were one of those examples. Thousands and thousands of young teen girls were strongly encouraged to learn to fly, parachute, participate in quasi-military skills, and shoot a variety of guns. Why were these skills necessary for young teens, especially girls, if the government did not plan to utilize them when they were fully trained? Young girls who desired further flight training and education in the flight schools were often denied acceptance. This did not make sense! Was the mandate for youngsters to attend Osoaviakhim just government propaganda to show the world they practiced gender equality education?

On the other hand, the published socialist ideology of the new Soviet woman was one of a modern, independent young woman working as an educated professional or as an uneducated factory worker. The nurturing domestic woman symbolized the love and caring of the land, Mother Russia. The key word here is "working." All women, young and old were to work for the government in one way or another before, during and after the war. Obviously, women had to be a bit confused especially after the Germans attacked. Were they supposed to be pilots, sharp shooters, chemists, teachers or stay at home mothers or farmers under the Stalin regime? If the women were trained to fly and shoot, why was the Stalin regime now publicly turning them away? At that point, Marina Raskova changed history once again by becoming involved and twisting Stalin's arm, so to speak.

There are conflicting theories as to why Stalin finally approved Marina Raskova's plan for the three women's air regiments. All seem to involve the public persona of what Stalin wanted personally and what he wanted the public to know. The theories are confusing, somewhat irrational, but typical of Stalin at the time:

1. The governmental perception to the citizens was that of a shortage of male pilots. In fact, there was not a shortage of pilots, there was a severe shortage of aircraft after the German's initial surprise attack wiped out a large portion of the available, airworthy aircraft.

2. Nationwide recruitment posters shouted, "The Motherland Is Calling." The posters were seemingly a call-to-arms for the Soviet women to join forces and fight for the Motherland even though Stalin did not want the world to know he would utilize women in front line combat. Perhaps this was a Stalin propaganda tactic to show gender equality was alive and well in the Soviet Union? Nonetheless, it was confusing to women as well as men.

3. The overwhelming national popularity of Marina Raskova and her public persistence/insistence that women be utilized to fight for the Motherland in front line aerial combat placed Stalin in an uncomfortable position. He had recognized and honored Raskova as a national hero, the entire nation loved and worshiped her. Would he dare not support her and what she wanted to do for the Motherland?

In a 1990 interview with author Anne Noggle *(A Dance with Death),* navigator Yevgeniya Guruleva-Smirnova recalled how the two factors of the modern woman ideal and the Mother Russia nurturer finally came together for the good of the Motherland with Stalin's approval, "No other country in the world let women fly combat, but Stalin proclaimed that our women could do everything, could withstand anything! It was a kind of propaganda to show that Soviet women were equal to men and could fulfill any task, to show how mighty and strong we were. Women could not only bring babies into being, but could build hydroelectric plants, fly aircraft, and destroy the enemy. Even if Stalin hadn't let the girls fly we would have volunteered by the thousands for the army."

Whatever the theories were, the facts and recognition are at long last becoming known worldwide. The Germans acknowledged the Witches were precise, merciless and came from nowhere. After the war Soviet pilot Alexey Maresyev, a highly decorated fighter pilot awarded the HSU, described the women combat pilots: "It is hardly possible to overestimate the contribution made by Soviet women to our victory over Nazism...many of them fell on the battlefield, having discharged their soldierly duty honorably. They had a zest for life; they wanted to study, to raise children, and to work hard, but when the need arose they faced danger and died without faltering. They consciously sacrificed their young lives in the great cause...onboard fighters and bombers they fought the enemy every bit as well as men did. These Soviet young girls amply demonstrated their iron will, steady hand, and accurate eye."

The French pilots from the Normandie-Niemen Regiment were also great admirers of the Soviet women pilots during the war. In 1960 they held a regimental reunion at Moscow's House of Friendship and warmly invited the surviving women pilots to attend. Jacques Andre, one of the highly decorated pilots from the regiment, gave the women a special presentation which read: "Fraternal greetings to my comrades-in-arms, young Soviet airwomen, who proved themselves men's equals in valor while fighting against the common enemy."

Major Valentin Markov, Commander of the 587th regiment after Marina Raskova's death, initially was not well liked or welcomed by the women pilots as he was unsure of their capabilities, "I couldn't visualize how I could command women during war, flying bombers. I knew the aircraft and knew how difficult it was even for men to fly. I didn't know how women could manage it." Likewise, he was not happy being appointed the position as their commander. Markov was a very strict, by-the-book military man who treated the women the same as the men in the regiment. After the war, during an interview he recalled, "The women in my regiment were self-disciplined, careful, and obedient to orders; they respected the truth and fair treatment toward them. They never whimpered and never complained and were very courageous. Almost all of them were shot down and, after hospitalization, they came back and flew bravely. If I compare my experience of commanding the male and female regiments, to some extent at the end of the war it was easier for me to command the female regiment. They had the strong spirit of a collective unit." Markov also felt the women in his regiment did not receive the recognition they were due (the HSU award), "From the present viewpoint I can see that very few of my girls were awarded the highest title. If I could turn time back, I would have promoted more of them for that award. Now I have a grave sentiment about that, because many of them deserved it."

Rumors that Stalin did not want the world to know he and his military commanders had women on the front lines in the air as well as on the ground, were likely the source and reason for the speech mentioned earlier telling the military women to "go home and be quiet" about their wartime experiences. With the passing of time and leadership, many of the women were no longer fearful of speaking out or writing about their thoughts and experiences. One such outspoken veteran was Mariya Smirnova, a former commander of one of the Night Witches' regiments. In later interviews she denied the brutality of war changed the women, made them callous or hardened. Instead their experiences and comradeship gave them a deeper appreciation and zest for life, "There is an opinion about women in combat that a woman stops being a woman after bombing, destroying, and killing; that she becomes crude and tough. This is not true; we all remained kind, compassionate, and loving. We became even more womanly, more caring of our children, our parents, and the land that has nourished us."

When Raskova's three regiments were deactivated at the end of the war, the women pledged to meet every year on May 2nd at the small park in front of Moscow's Bolshoi Theater. They welcomed each other with open arms at the

An annual gathering of the remaining regimental sestry, date undetermined.

sight of their *sestry,* sisters, sharing stories, singing songs, celebrating their survival and paying tribute to those who were lost during and after the war. The three groups would then split off into their former regiments for lunch and further reminiscing. As the years slipped by, many of the women passed away but those still able, continued to meet at the same location every year.

In the United States after the war was declared over, the WASP (Women Airforce Service Pilots) were also being deactivated, with the same misgivings experienced by the Witches; they wanted to continue flying, either in the military or civilian skies but had barriers thrown up against them. Many fought successfully to become pilots for commercial operations or flying the mail, while others resorted to simply flying for their own pleasure. In any case the WASP began having their own reunions just as the Witches did.

As many of the U.S. bomber pilots returned from the European theater, their stories of the Soviet Night Witches and their amazing, fearless accomplishments began to surface. The WASP heard the stories and held the Witches in awe. It was difficult to comprehend why the Soviet government allowed their women to fly combat missions while the U.S. government restricted American women pilots to noncombat, aircraft ferrying missions. Politics - no doubt.

Very little, if any, communication between the two groups of women took place during this time period due to the Cold War and reconstruction efforts. As the Cold War thawed and the political climate changed, more information about the Night Witches found its way to the WASP and vice versa. On May 2, 1990 a group of forty former WASPs traveled to Moscow to meet the remaining Night Witches at the park in front of the Bolshoi Theater. The meeting was of great historical significance as the world's first female military pilots met each other for the first time. The first thing the two groups of women discovered about each other was both had an overwhelming desire to fly aircraft and do so in defense of their respective countries. Each group had strong ties to each other after surviving the stress of training, flying, and wartime duties. They were ALL sisters! Barbara Lazarsky, president of the WASP at that time, was quoted as saying to the group, "We are grateful to you for having been our allies. We hope to remain friends." Marion Hodgson, another WASP attending, later wrote, "For us the Cold War ended that May."

Former WASP, author Anne Noggle was one of those attending that first gathering. Anne returned to the Soviet Union that fall to interview and photograph sixty-nine of the remaining Night Witches for her book, *A Dance With Death*. Published in 1994, she penned the following in her preface:

"I thought then, on my way to their country, that these stories would cut across all boundaries and that our gender-relatedness was a key - our sameness as girls and women, past and present would be more significant than

our differing cultural backgrounds. That proved to be true. As they told their stories, their voices and gestures spoke even before the translated words. For people held mute for almost all the years of their lives by terror and despotism, the communication of the spirit has never been silenced."

On June 18, 2005, the San Diego Aerospace Museum hosted an all day symposium which featured five women who had served in the Soviet Army Air Regiments during WWII. Each of the five women spoke to the gathering about their wartime experiences, with assistance from a translator. Representing the 588th Bomber Regiment, the Night Witches, was Nadezhda (Nadia) Popova pilot, perhaps the most outspoken even at age eighty-four; from the 586th Fighter Regiment Tamara Pamiatnykh pilot and Squadron Commander; Ekaterina Polunina, Senior Mechanic and Regiment historian; Galina Brok-Bel'tsova Navigator-Bombardier; and Anna Kirilina Armament Mechanic. It was a memorable day for all involved!

The Flying Heritage Collection (an aviation museum) in Everett, Washington has a beautifully restored Po-2 aircraft like the ones flown by the 588th Night Witches. It also has an Il-2 (Ilyushin Sturmovick) like the one flown by Anna Yegorova. A German Messerschmidt, the planes that tried to shoot the Witches from the sky in order to receive their Iron Cross award from Hitler, is also on display. All of these planes, and many others on display, are flyable and participate in frequent flight events at the Museum.

A restored Po-2 flown by the Night Witches.
Photo credit: Flying Heritage Collection.

Restored Soviet Il-2. Photo by E. Hagen

Restored German Messerschmidt. Photo by E. Hagen

The Night Witches were one of the most extraordinary, historically significant female fighting forces of WWII. There was no witchcraft involved! The young women volunteered to be a part of this military force and did what they could for the love of their country and did it well. Now that more information is being exchanged between the two countries we hope to hear/read more about these women and their significance in WWII history.

At their annual gatherings on May 2 in Moscow the women would toast a shot of vodka to each other:

"To women, to pilots, WE ARE ONE!"

Few if any of these amazing women are alive today.

Acknowledgements

This was an interesting book to research and write! With each book I write, I learn something different whether it is in the writing itself, the publishing process, or the subject matter. For this book I learned how important it is to investigate every detail and statistic then double check again in multiple sources. There is a saying that it might take a week or a month of research and fact checking to write a single line or paragraph. That statement proved true time and time again for this book.

Many people encouraged me along the way by simply stating they had never heard of the Soviet Night Witches. It became my mission to change that! Thanks to my husband Ernie Hagen for his WWII aviation expertise, photography and computer help. My editor Julie Cline for taking the reins during difficult times of her own to accomplish this epic job. To Jennifer Bicek for her content edit and thoughtful review. To Marty Bicek for creating the eye catching cover. And special thanks to all my exercise buddies who frequently asked, "is it done yet?"

Bibliography

Articles

"Airwomen of the Red Star: Soviet Combat Veterans of World War II Symposium." *Aero News Network.* May 4, 2005.

Aldrich, Nancy W., Captain. "Marina Raskova." *20th Century Aviation* magazine.com. 2013.

Aldrich, Nancy W., Captain. "The Witch is Dead." *20th Century Aviation Magazine.com.* 20013.

"Ekaterina Budanova. How she became the heroic woman pilot." *Rus Articles Journal.* May 3, 2016.

"Flying Into the Past." *Southern Living Magazine.* 1998.

Garber, Megan. "Night Witches: The Female Fighter Pilots of World War II." *The Atlantic.* July 15, 2013.

Gibson, Karen Bush. "Valentina Grizodubova: The Soviet Amelia Earhart." *Gizmodo.* July 29, 2013.

Green, Kim. "Russian Women Combat Pilots." *Woman Pilot.* July 18, 2012.

Green, Kim. "The White Rose of Stalingrad." *Woman Pilot.* July 18, 2012.

Harris, Adrienne Marie. "The Myth of the Woman Warrior and World War II Soviet Culture." University of Kansas. 2001.

Henderson, Suzy. "The Night Witches." *Blog: Wartime Wednesdays.* September 17, 2014.

Hull, Michael. "The Red Air Force's Female Fighter Ace Lily Litvak." *Warfare History Network.* November 17, 2015.

Bibliography

Articles (continued)

Klayman, Alison. "The Night Witches."
The New York Times - Opinion Pages.
December 19, 2013.

Krylov, Aleksander. "WWII: The Decisive Role of the
Russian People in Defeating Nazi Germany"
(translated from Russian May 12, 2007).
Global Research.

Markowitz, Mike. "Night Witches: Soviet Female Aviators
in World War II." *Defense Media Network.*
May 7, 2014.

Markwick, Roger. "Irina Rakobolskaya obituary." *The
Guardian.* October 16, 2016.

Martin, Douglas. "Nadezhda Popova, WWII Night Witch,
Dies at 91." *The New York Times.* July 14, 2013.

Miller, Daniel. "The 'Night Witch' who carried out
hundreds of bombing raids as part of Russia's
elite all-women World War II air squad."
Daily Mail. July 11, 2013.

Monahan, Maureen. "The Lethal Soviet 'Night Witches'
of the 588th Night Bomber Unit." *Mental Floss.*
July 26, 2013.

"Nadia Popova." *The Economist.* April 20, 2013.

Pennington, Reina. "Not just Night Witches."
Air Force Magazine. October, 2014.

Spurling, Kathryn. "A True Adventure."
H-Minerva, H-Net Reviews. July, 2002.

Bibliography

Articles (continued)

Taylor, Alan. "World War II: The Eastern Front."
   The Atlantic. September 18, 2011.

"The Rodina." *Historic Wings Flight Stories.*
   September 24, 2012.

Valigursky, Michelle. "To Women, To Pilots, We Are One."
   Emory Wire Magazine. December 2012.

Wilson, George Tipton. "The Red Air Force Night Witches:
   Flight of the Rodina." *Warfare History.*
   December 26, 2015.

Books

Breuer, William B. *Unexplained Mysteries of World War II.*
   Castle Books. 1997.

Bergstrom, Christer & Mikhailov, Andrey. *Soviet Night
   Witches Over the Caucasus.* Bergstrom Books.
   2000-2001.

Cottam, K. Jean. *Soviet Airwomen in Combat in World War
   II.* Manhattan, Kansas: Sunflower University Press,
   1983.

Cottam, K. Jean. *Women in War & Resistance Selected
   Biographies of Soviet Women Soldiers.*
   New Military Publishing. 1998.

Cottam, K. Jean. *Women in Air War: The Eastern Front in
   World War II.* Newburyport: Focus Publishing. 1998.

Hagen, Claudia. *American Women During WWII.*
   CreateSpace. 2015.

Bibliography

Books (continued)

Kelly, Martha Hall. *Lilac Girls*. Ballantine Books. 2016.

Lord, Walter. *Day of Infamy.* Henry Holt & Co. 1957.

Markwick, Roger & Cardona, Euridice Charon. *Soviet Women on the Frontline in the Second World War.* Palgrove MacMillan. 2012.

Mason, Fergus. *Night Witches.* Bookcaps. 2014.

McCormack, S.J. *Night Witch.* CreateSpace. 2015.

McShane, Roy. *HWELTE. The Best Kept Russian Secret of World War II.* Universe. 2002.

Myles, Bruce. *Night Witches. The Amazing Story of Russia's Women Pilots in World War II.* Academy Chicago Publishers. 1990.

Noggle, Anne. *A Dance With Death. Soviet Airwomen in World War II.* Texas A&M University Press. 1994.

Parrish, Thomas (editor). *The Simon and Schuster Encyclopedia of World War II.* Simon & Schuster. 1978.

Pennington, Reina. *Wings, Women, & War. Soviet Air women in World War II Combat.* University Press of Kansas. 2001.

Schrader, Helena Page. *Sisters in Arms.* Pen & Sword Books Ltd. 2006.

Strebe Goodpaster, Amy. *Flying For Her Country.* Potomac Books, Inc. 2009.

Timofeyeva-Yegorova, Anna. *Red Sky, Black Death. A Soviet Woman Pilot's Memoir of the Eastern Front.* Slavica Publishers. 2009.

Bibliography

Books (continued)

Yenne, Bill. *The White Rose of Stalingrad. The real life adventures of Lidya Vladimirovna Litvyak, the highest scoring female Air Ace of all time.* Osprey Publishing, Great Britain. 2013.

Websites/Webpages

"Ace Profile - Major Marina Mikhailovna Raskova." August 25, 2014. March 16, 2016.
reddit.com/r/warthunder/comments/2eixmt/ace_profile_major_marina_mikhailovna_raskova/

Andrews, Evan. "8 things you should know about WWII's Eastern Front." 2014. November 8, 2015.
history.com/news/history-lists/8-things-you-should-know-about-wwuus-eastern-front/print

"A Hero You May Have Missed - Nachthexen." July 17, 2013. November 8, 2015.
stripersonline.com/surftalk/topic/541833-a-he

"Anna Yegorova." May 17, 2016.
badassoftheweek.com/yegorova.html

Chen, Peter C. "Yekaterina Budanova." September 15, 2011. May 3, 2016.
2db.com/peron_bio.php?person_id=645

Chen, Peter C. "Caucasus Campaign July 23, 1942 - October 9, 1943." April 20, 2016.
2db.com/battle_spec.php?battle_id=284

Bibliography

Websites/Webpages (continued)

"Difference Between Soviet Union and Russia."
January 26, 2016.
differencebetween.net/miscellaneous/politics/political-institutions/difference-between-soviet-union-and-russia

Dowdy, Linda. "The Night Witches - The True Story
of an Incredible Group of Women."
February 11, 2016.
seizethesky.com/nwitches/nite.wtch.html

Duncan, Phyllis-Anne. "Russian Women Pilots."
November 3, 2015.
avstop.com/history/aroundtheworld/russia/nexen.htm

Dykman, J.T. "WWII Soviet Experience."
January 26, 2016.
eisenhowerinstitute.org/about/living.history/wwii_soviet_experience.dot

Ellman, Michael & Maksudov, S. "Soviet Deaths in the
Great Patriotic War: A Note." March 5, 2016.
sovietinfo.tripod.com

"Female Badasses in History: Ann Timofeyeva-Yegorova
(1916-2009)." February 18, 2012. May 17, 2016.
spaceinvaderjoe.wordpress.com/category/world-war-ii/

"German-Soviet Nonaggression Pact." March 8, 2016.
history.com/topics/world-war-ii/german-soviet-nonaggression-pact/print

Bibliography

Websites/Webpages (continued)

Gibson, Karen Bush. "Valentina Grizodubova: The Soviet
    Amelia Earhart." July 29, 2013. March 14, 2016.
    gizmodo.com/valentina-grizodubova-the-soviet-amelia-
    earhart-887771077

Grundhauser, Eric. "The Little-Known Story of the Night
    Witches, an all Female Force in WWII."
    June 25, 2015. November 3, 2015.
    vanityfair.com/culture/2015/06/night-witches-
    wwii-female-pilots

"Joseph Stalin." 2009. March 7, 2016.
    history.com/topics/joseph-stalin/print

Kamenir, Victor. "Breaching the Blue Line: The Soviet
    Army at the Taman Peninsula." 2014. April 20, 2016.
    warfarehistorynetwork.com/daily/wwii/breaching-the-blue-line-
    the-soviet-army-at-the-taman-peninsula/print/

Keefe, Joshua R. "Stalin and the Drive to Industrialize the
    Soviet Union." 2009. March 8, 2016.
    studentpulse.com/print?id=8

Kirkhart, Hannah. "Nachthexen." May 28, 2016.
    baylor.edu/content/services/document.php/177359.doc

Kozhedub, Ivan. "Aviation History: Interview with World
    War II Soviet Ace Ivan Kozhedub." Aviation History.
    June 12, 2006. March 13, 2016.
    historynet.com/aviation-history-interview-with-world-war-ii-
    soviet-ace-ivan-kozhedub.htm

Bibliography

Websites/Webpages (continued)

Lee, Michelle. "Irina Feodorovan Sebrova."
September, 2013.
michellesworldhistoryhomework.blogspot.com/
2013/09/i-am-feodorovna-sebrova-i-was-female.html

"Lieutenant Anna Alexandrovna Timofeyeva Yegorova."
March 19, 2016.
findagrave.com/cgi-bin/fg.cgi?page=gr&GRid=52260557

"Marina Raskova and the Night Witches." March 29, 2016.
25106262.weebly.com/legacy.html

"Marina Raskova and the Soviet Women Pilots of World
War II." November 15, 2015.
ctie.monash.edu.au/hargrave/soviet_women_pilots.html

Markwick, Roger. "Irina Rakobolskaya obituary."
October 16, 2016.
theguardian.com/world/2016/oct/16/irina-rakobolskaya-obituary

"Night Witches - Nachthexen." March 9, 2015.
November 8, 2015. sonocarina.wordpress.com/tag/ww2

Pennington, Reina. "Inna Pasportnikova, 1920-2007."
2015. June 4, 2016. lilyalitviak.org/styled-21/styled-2/

"Russia Beyond the Headlines-WWII."
November 15, 2015. rbth.com/wwii

"Russia in World War 2." November 15, 2015.
2worldwar2.com/russia.htm

Bibliography

Websites/Webpages (continued)

"Russian History: The Great Patriotic War."
November 15, 2015.
russiapedia.rt.com/russian-history/the-great-patriotic-war/

"Soviet Female Night Bomber WW2 Pilots."
November 8, 2015. wio.ru/aces/gal-f.htm

"Soviet Union Air Defense, 586th Fighter Aviation
Regiment (Combatants/Military Personnel)
May24, 2016.
what-when-how.com/women-and-war/soviet-union-air-defense-586th-fighter-aviation-regiment-combatantsmilitary-personnel/

"Soviet Union, 46th Taman Guards Bomber Aviation
Regiment (Combatants/Military Personnel).
May 25, 2016.
what-when-how.com/women-and-war/soviet-union-46th-taman-guards-bomber-aviation-regiment-combatantsmilitary-personnel/

Stockton, Harold E., Tyminski, Dariusz, Bergstrom,
Christer. August, 1995.
"Marina Raskova and Soviet Female Pilots."
November 15, 2015. acestory.elknet.pl/raskov/raskov.htm

Swopes, Bryan. "This Day in Aviation: 24-25,
September 1938. September 25, 2015.
thisdayinaviation.com/24-25-september-1938/

"The 588th Bomber Regiment, or The Night Witches."
March 29, 2016.
25106262.weebly.com/the-night-witches.html

Bibliography

Websites/Webpages (continued)

"The Beginning of Soviet Civil Aviation." March 12, 2016.
centennialofflight.net/essay/commerecial_aviation/
soviet_air/tran17.htm

"The Female Soldier Marina Raskova." October 4, 2015.
March 24, 2016.
thefemalesoldier.com/blog/marina-raskova

"The Great Patriotic War." November 15, 2015.
marxists.org/history/ussr/great-patriotic-war/

"The Night Witches - Russian Combat Pilots of
World War Two. December 5, 2005. April 13, 2016.
h2g2.com/approved_entry/A5849076

"The Rodina." Historic Wings Online Magazine.
September 24, 2012. July 22, 2016.
fly.historicwings.com

"Timeline of Operation Bagration (June-August 1944).
2006-2016. April 22, 2016.
secondworldwarhistory.com/operation-bagration.asp

"Transport in the Soviet Union Explained."
March 12, 2016.
everything.explained.today/transport_in_the_soviet-union

Truman, C.N. "German Night Fighters." May 19, 2015,
December 16, 2015. January 15, 2016.
history/earningsite.com.uk/world-war-two/the-bombing-cam
paign-of-world-war-two/german-night-fighters/

Bibliography

Websites/Webpages (continued)

Wilson, George Tipton. "Red Air Force Heroines: The
Night Witches." September 16, 2016.
warfarehistorynetwork.com/daily/wwii/red-air-force-
heroines-the-night-witches/print/

"World War 2 Insightful Essays." (Multiple links:
WW2 summary; WW2 Casualties; Causes of WW2;
The turning points of WW2; Russia in WW2; Time
line; Stalingrad; Knights Cross). January 11, 2016.
2worldwar2.com

Wikipedia
*(Note: The topics listed below were the search subjects. Links to
their original sources were previously listed if utilized. Dates
searched are listed with time of search in military time).*

8.8 cm Flak 18/36/37/41 - November 8, 2015 - 12:01.

Adolf Hitler - March 11, 2016 - 12:04.

Aftermath of World War II - July 27, 2016 - 15:42.

Alexey Maresyev - August 13, 2016 - 12:30.

Anna Yegorova - November 9, 2015 - 15:25,
May 17, 2016 - 17:24, May 19, 2016 - 13:04.

Anti-aircraft warfare - July 2, 2016 - 12:45.

Aviation and the purges - March 13, 2016 -15:48.

Aviation between the World Wars - March 12, 2016 - 15:02.

Bibliography

Wikipedia (continued)

Conspiracy theories about Adolf Hitler's death - November 12, 2016 - 15:11.

DOSAAF (OSOAVIAKhIM) - March 13, 2016 - 12:57, 16:12.

End of World War II in Europe - July 27, 2016 - 15:42.

Extraordinary State Commission for Ascertaining and Investigating Crimes Perpetrated by the German-Fascist Invaders - April 29, 2016 - 13:14.

Great Patriotic War (term) November 15, 2015 - 14:17.

Guards Unit - September 10, 2016 - 09:31.

Hero of the Soviet Union - March 13, 2016 - 12:50.

Ilyushin Il-2 - May 18, 2016 - 15:52.

Irina Sebrova - May 27, 2016 - 13:58.

Joseph Kociok - April 19, 2016 - 16:18.

Joseph Stalin - March 7, 2016 - 15:29.

Komsomol - November 15, 2015 - 12:52.

List of German WWII Night Fighter Aces - January 15, 2016 - 13:15.

List of Russian Aviators - July 6, 2016 - 15:44.

Lisunov Li-2 - August 31, 2016 - 13:16.

Little Octoberists - March 18, 2016 - 12:58

Bibliography

Wikipedia (continued)

Lydia Litvyak - November 9, 2015 - 14:32.

Marina Raskova - November 8, 2015 - 12:22.

Moscow Victory Parade of 1945 - July 27, 2016 - 15:14.

Nadezhda Popova - November 8, 2015 - 12:36.

Night Witches - April 27, 2016 - 10:39, July 2, 2016 - 15:48.

Operation Bagration - April 22, 2016 - 13:09.

Operation Barbarossa - February 4, 2016 - 14:51.

Polikarpov Po-2 - November 8, 2015 - 12:13.

Ranks and Rank Insignia of the Red Army 1940-1943 - June 6, 2016 - 11:57.

Russia - March 4, 2016 - 14:05.

ShKAS Machine Gun - August 11, 2016 - 14:10.

Soviet Air Forces - March 12, 2016 - 13:03.

Soviet Partisans - April 29, 2016 - 11:20.

Soviet Women in World War II - November 9, 2015 - 14:15.

Soviet Union - March 4, 2016 - 13:55.

Tracer Ammunition - July 26, 2016 - 12:26.

Valentina Grizodubova - April 9, 2016 - 15:02.

Bibliography

Wikipedia (continued)

Vladimir Lenin All-Union Pioneer Organization -
    March 18, 2016 - 15:08.

Wartime Homefront - January 26, 2016 - 13:09.

Women in the Russian and Soviet Military -
    July 16, 2016 - 14:20.

World War II Casualties of the Soviet Union -
    March 5, 2016 - 15:02, August 3, 2016 - 13:30.

Yevdokia Bershanskaya - March 30, 2016 - 12:38.

Yekaterina Budanova - May 3, 2016 - 14:50.

Films/Videos

"Apocalypse - The Second World War."
    Smithsonian Channel. March 6, 2016.

"Call Sign White Lily." Interview with Valentina
    Vaschenko at the Lilya Litvyak Museum.
    August 4, 2016.

"Night Witches." Parts one through six. Film by Gunilla
    Bresky. Published February 27, 2013.
    November 20, 2015.

"Sisters. An Original Documentary Treatment." Slide show.
    McShane Websites. November 18, 2015.

"Night Witches. Soviet Airwomen in WWII." Documentary
    newsreel. August 16, 2009. November 20, 2015.

Bibliography

Films/Videos (continued)

"The Night Witch: The Story of Nadia, Soviet Bomber
	Pilot." OP-Docs/The New York Times via YouTube.
	Published February 27, 2013. November 20, 2015.

About the Author

"Tonight We Fly!" The Soviet Night Witches of WWII is the fifth non-fiction book by author Claudia Hagen. *American Women During WWII, The Night A Fortress Fell To Fairfield, The Mystic High Adventures of Fannie Flame & Crew,* and *Hanford's Secret Clouds of Despair* were her first published works along with her first children's book, *Our Grandma Flies A Hot Air Balloon* followed by *Keely The Rescued Kitty.*

After thirty-six years as a critical care nurse and twelve years as a commercially rated hot air balloon pilot, she is now retired and living in California's Central Valley. When she is not researching or writing she enjoys reading, gardening and traveling.

Learn more about Claudia and her books at:
www.claudiahagen.com

Made in the
USA
Columbia, SC